Play and Learn

from Two
to
Three Years

Dedication

We would like to dedicate this book to Stephen, Karen and Lauren, children of Susan Talpins, in appreciation of their generosity in lending us their mother.

Play and Learn

Volume III

from Two to Three Years

By Don Adcock & Marilyn Segal

OAK TREE PUBLICATIONS, INC.
PUBLISHERS, LA JOLLA, CALIFORNIA

Play and Learn: From Two to Three Years
©copyright 1980 by Oak Tree Publications. First
edition ©1979 by Nova University. All rights reserved
under International and Pan American Copyright
Conventions. No part of this book may be reproduced
in any manner whatsoever without written permission
from the publisher, except in the case of brief
quotations embodied in reviews and articles.

Second Edition
Manufactured in the United States of America
For information write to : Oak Tree Publications, Inc.,
P.O. Box 1012 La Jolla, CA 92038

Library of Congress Cataloging in Publication Data
Adcock, Don.
  Play and learn, from two to three years.

  1. Play. 2. Child development. I. Segal, Marilyn
M., joint author. II. Title. III. Title: From two
to three years.
HQ782.A32   1980   155.4'18   80-13834
ISBN 0-916392-52-X (pbk.)

1 2 3 4 5 6 7 8 9   84 83 82 81 80

Preface

Two-year-olds are the subject of this third volume in the "Play & Learn" series. The development of social behavior and learning skills are the major topics. It is based on a study of eighty-six two-year-old children and their families conducted through the Institute of Child Centered Education at Nova University. The primary vehicle for gathering information was home visits, through which the staff had an opportunity to observe the natural interplay of parents and children, to identify different parenting styles, to record behaviors and to collect anecdotes and the candid photos that illustrate this book.

Not all the concepts and skills that two-year-olds learn can be discussed in a single book. "Explorations" discusses the various ways in which a two-year-old explores his environment. "Imagination" describes different styles of pretending and explores the role of the adult in encouraging imaginative play. "Learning Through Language" describes three major facets of early language development. It is important to remember that typical development represents an average. Some children will be ahead of this average and some will be behind. The "typical child" is an abstraction and our descriptions of typical development can never form a perfect match with real children.

We concentrate on the social development of two-year-olds because this age is a pivotal year in development. Children are mastering the art of communicating, they are learning to play with children, they are exploring the world with new skills, and they are developing a sense of imagination and humor. The outcome is a definition of self. We take a close look at this self-definition in the hope of identifying some of the major factors that influence the personal growth of two-year-olds.

We do not believe there is one right way to bring up children, however, we do believe strongly that parents should discover the methods that they are comfortable with while taking into account the special nature of their own children. Throughout this book we talk about routine problems that are a part of living with two-year-olds, and we describe some of the creative ways that the parents found to cope with these everyday problems. In addition to sharing ideas on child rearing, we hope to provide the reader with a sampling of two-year-old behavior. Another reason for writing this book is to increase the pleasure that parents receive from their children.

Acknowledgments

We would like to extend a very special thank you to Susan Talpins, Research Associate at Nova University, who played a major role in the planning, data collection and conceptualization of this book. She worked hand in hand with the authors from the first contact with parents through the final proofing of the galleys. Her insights, criticisms and fantastic memory made her indispensable.

We would also like to thank Fleurette Aranow and Elizabeth Ann Kalb for their invaluable help in collating and organizing the mountains of data collected in the study.

And finally, a special thank you to the 86 parents and their children who participated in the study. In a very real sense these families are our co-authors.

Part 1: Play and Learning

Contents

Chapter I—Explorations 1
Visual Exploration 4
   Looking for Things 4
   Watching for Changes 5
Filling and Emptying 6
   Exploring Containers 6
Puzzles 7
   Pouring and Mixing 8
Drawing and Building 10
   Drawing 10
   Building 12
   Arts and Crafts 14
   Machines 15
   Mechanical Toys 17
   Tools 18
Moving Through Space 20
   Exploration with Movement 20
   Action Games 25
   Going Places 26
   Summary 28

Chapter II—Imagination 31
Developmental Advances 33
Individual Differences 35
   The Actor Style 36
   Producer-Director Style 45
Reasons for Pretending 48
   Making Sense Out of the World 48
   Compensating for Feelings of Inadequacy ...49

Ways to Foster Imaginative Play 52
   The Role of the Adult 52
   The Props 56
   Things to Put On 56
   Things To Travel On 56
   Places To Go To 57
   Things To Carry 57
   Things To Use 57
   Playscapes 58
   Miniature Type Props 58
   Raw Materials 58
   Play Space 59
   Summary 59

Chapter III—Learning Through Language ..61
   Learning To Listen 63
   Listening Activities 64
   Listening To Television 65
Reading and Listening 66
   Suggestions For Reading 68
   Teaching Two-Year-Olds To Read 69
   Learning To Converse 69
   The Transition From Inflection To Words ..71
   Combining Words Into Sentences 72
   Learning To Converse 73
   Affecting Another Person's Behavior ...74
   Communicating Ideas 76
Conversational Play and Humor 79
Concluding Thought—The Role of Parents ...80

Chapter I—Explorations

Visual Exploration	4
Looking for Things	4
Watching for Changes	5
Filling and Emptying	6
Exploring Containers	6
Puzzles	7
Pouring and Mixing	8
Drawing and Building	10
Drawing	10
Building	12
Arts and Crafts	14
Machines	15
Mechanical Toys	17
Tools	18
Moving Through Space	20
Exploration with Movement	20
Action Games	25
Going Places	26
Summary	28

Chapter I
Explorations

Lisa looked up quickly as her mother entered the bedroom.

"Lisa, what are you doing with that good perfume?... Oh, no! You naughty girl — You poured it all out."

Lisa's mother was too upset to explain her feelings any further. She gave Lisa a good spanking and sent her to her room. "Things like this always seem to happen when I'm on the phone," she thought to herself. "And why didn't I have the sense to put that perfume in a safer place?"

Exploration means playing with objects, and learning about them in the process. As soon as they are able, children start to explore the world by manipulating the objects around them. Their ability to explore grows as they become stronger, more coordinated, and more determined. By the age of two children are not easily deterred from their goals. Lisa wanted to play with the perfume, and she knew exactly when to go into her mother's bedroom and how to get up on the dresser. It was hard to get the little cap unscrewed, but her perseverance had been rewarded.

There are moments when every parent is upset by a child's exploration. It seems that exploration always means playing with things that are off limits. It certainly is true that two year old children tend to be most interested in the very objects they are not allowed to play with. Lisa's mother was particularly angry because she felt that Lisa knew better than to play with the perfume. It seemed like defiance on Lisa's part, defiance of a restriction that was reasonable.

The exploration of two year olds can turn into defiance. The children are sophisticated enough to tease a parent, or even to get back at a parent, by getting into things they shouldn't. In extreme cases children are involved continually in this kind of rebellion. They seem to see the world in terms of confrontation, and they build up their sense of accomplishment by breaking the limits parents set. If they are not caught, their sense of accomplishment is built up by the feeling that something has been put over on the adults. And if they are caught, at least they have succeeded in getting their parents' attention.

However, not all inappropriate exploration is an expression of defiance. Lisa may have merely succumbed to temptation, as we all do at times. Perhaps she was trying to imitate her mother by putting on some perfume. A forbidden object often is explored not so much because it is forbidden but because it represents a chance to imitate adults, to participate in the grown-up world.

There is a subtle but unmistakable difference in emphasis between the exploration of the 1-2 year old as against the 2-3 year old. By two years children are less concerned with experimentation and more concerned about mastering skills. Instead of trying a whole bag of manipulative tricks on an object, the two year old child practices skills associated with that object. Kim, for example, was very interested in exploring her mother's lipstick. Most of the time she did not try to squash the lipstick, break it into pieces, or smear it on the walls. Instead she practiced making the lipstick go up and down in the tube and spreading it on her lips.

Exploration has two faces. When we look at it one way, we see the possibility of conflict between children and parents, as they clash over restrictions and rules. When we look at its other face, we see the possibility of cooperation as children learn from their parents how to master certain manipulative skills. Use of the perfume bottle may become a recurring battle at Lisa's house, or it may become a learning opportunity. Perhaps Lisa could put on a drop of perfume while her mother supervised, or perhaps she could have her own bottle of inexpensive perfume to put on as she likes. Then again, Lisa might refuse to accept these ideas and continue to sneak into her mother's bedroom during opportune moments. Some children seem to persist in a kind of one-track exploration no matter how their parents handle it.

Whether exploration leads to confrontation or cooperation depends on children as well as parents. Some children are especially independent, active, or curious. Some children don't understand verbal explanations their parents give them about the rules for exploration. The situation is different in every family. There is no one way for parents to substitute cooperation for confrontation, and even if families are relatively successful in avoiding confrontation, situations arise in which there is no way at all to avoid it. A certain amount of conflict over exploration is inevitable.

In this chapter we will describe some of the major ways two year olds explore their environment. The first section discusses visual exploration. Much of a child's time is spent just watching things, and although this is not a direct form of manipulation, it serves the same purpose. The next three sections look at situations in which children manipulate objects with their hands. They empty and fill containers, they draw and build, and they make things work (or make them so they won't work). In the final section we describe how children explore the world through other body movements, like running, jumping, and throwing. When we view the exploration of two year olds in this larger context, we see that most of the time children are not involved in furtive exploration. To be sure, there are times when their exploration is exasperating, but on the whole, it is a fascinating process for parents to observe.

Visual Exploration

Looking for Things When we think about the exploration of two year olds, we get a picture of incessant activity, running from one room to another, jumping on the bed, piling toys in the middle of the room. Exploration is all of this, but it is more besides. Even when

young children are sitting quietly they usually are exploring the world with their eyes. They are not involved in mental reflection, as adults often are, but are very much tuned in to the immediate environment.

Visual exploration occurs all the time, but it is most noticeable when children are restricted from moving around. The outstanding example is riding in the car. "I see a crane — Boy, that's a big one — Pow — splash", Stuart described the sound of the crane's bucket hitting the water as it dipped down to scoop up another load of gravel. When Stuart rode in the car, he was happy as long as a crane could be found every ten minutes or so. Luckily there were a lot of other gravel pits in the neighborhood.

When they left the neighborhood Stuart's parents found that they could encourage Stuart to look for other objects. He especially liked identifying gas station signs. The funny thing was that when they took the Interstate Highway, which was replete with interesting gas stations and vehicles, Stuart seemed very restless until they slowed down to exit.

Many children are like Stuart in that they look for particular objects while riding in the car. Helaine looked for cement mixers; Jennifer looked for big trees; Erik looked for fireboxes. This kind of behavior is another indication of how the exploration of the toddler turns into a sense of mastery in the two year old. Instead of just watching the scenery go by,

the children try to master the visual environment by actively searching for favorite sights. And like Stuart, if the scenery becomes too dull or starts to go by too quickly, the children lose interest in visual exploration. They lose the sense of being in control.

Searching for special objects also involves matching. The children are taking into account the similarities between objects. Matching is prominent at the dinner table where two year olds are more or less confined to their chairs. One night when company was coming, Jeff's mother set the table with dark green glasses, thinking that Jeff would be happy to get an adult glass instead of his usual plastic one. But Jeff was not fooled so easily. "I want beer," he announced as soon as the meal began. The white liquid in his glass obviously did not match the bubbly stuff in everyone else's glasses.

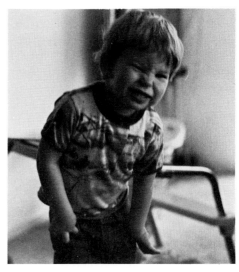

Matching often is stimulated by a negative presence, something undesirable that the child wants to avoid. Susan demonstrated her matching skill by fishing out the peas in her vegetable soup (and then dropping them ceremoniously on the floor). Chris, who was distressed about a hole in his pocket, checked all his other pockets, as well as his father's pockets, to see if they had holes. Erik did not like the way the label in one of his shirts rubbed against his neck. His mother would not agree to ruin the shirt by cutting out the label, even though Erik showed her the offensive labels in all his other shirts.

Watching for Changes

A number of parents reported that their children were interested in watching the sky. The sky is relatively uncluttered, and maybe this is why two year old children are attracted to it. Perhaps it is simply the majesty of the sky. In any event there are interesting objects in the sky. Two year olds are like toddlers in that they watch the movements of birds and airplanes. In addition many of them become attentive to clouds, the sun, and the moon.

A favorite spot for watching the sky seems to be sitting in a swing. Most two year olds have not really learned to pump the swing, and as an adult pushes them, they have ample opportunity for sky gazing. Swinging higher and higher, it must seem as if they are actually going up to meet the sky. Looking down is interesting too, especially on a sunny day. "I see the shadow," Nicole chanted to herself. "where you go shadow?", she playfully mused as the shadow passed out of sight beneath her feet, and then as it appeared again on the backswing. "I see you now — you silly shadow."

Shadows are mysterious phenomena that intrigue children once they are discovered. They change their shape on walls, grow long at night, and disappear altogether on some days. But they make good companions, always ready to play "Follow the Leader" and always right in step.

The world is full of physical changes that we take for granted but which two year old children see as fresh and exciting. One of the most common, and yet fascinating, is the movement of water down a drain. Some children develop a fear of going down the drain themselves, but it is more than fear that motivates children to watch drains. The water seems to move with a will of its own, carrying along an entourage of bubbles and bits of debris. Dropping a stone in a pool of water is similar. At first there is an interesting sound, a pfloop, and then the rock disappears, swallowed up in a pattern of ripples.

Melting is another surprising event. Stephanie watched the ice cube disappearing in her bowl of soup. Ice cubes in soup was a ritual at her house, ever since the first time Stephanie had burned her mouth on hot soup. Now Stephanie asked for the ice cube even when she didn't want to eat the soup. Andrew watched the burning candle fill up with melted wax and then drip slowly down the side. From repeated burnings the base of the candle looked like a multicolored waterfall. Andrew wanted to touch the wax as it assumed its new shape at the bottom of the candle, but he had learned from past experience just to watch.

Probably the most dramatic physical change two year olds watch is bleeding. Suddenly bright red liquid covers the skin, emerging effortlessly from a break that often is not visible. Again, many children eventually develop a fear of blood, but more frequently the reaction among two year olds is one of fascination. As Jenny exclaimed when she saw the blood from a cut on her leg, "What is *that?*". She wanted to know where it came from and listened attentively to a brief description of her insides. Thinking that her father would be just as overwhelmed by the discovery of blood, she kept telling her mother all afternoon, "I want to show Daddy when he gets home."

Not as dramatic, but still interesting, is the scab formed by dried blood. Two year old children are forever on the lookout for scratches and scrapes on themselves and other people. Some children discover that by picking at a scab, they can make the blood flow again. Scabs are special body parts that come and go. Each one serves as a conversation piece for a few days and then fades away. Erik wondered about the disappearance of a scab one day, and then concluded that it must have gone down the bathtub drain. It had been washed away with soap and water.

Watching for scabs is part of a larger pattern — noting parts of the body. By two years of age many children seem to realize that human beings share certain features, such as hands, feet and parts of the face. Michael, for example, pointed out a similarity by going around the room at Thanksgiving and touching the nose of everyone present. Michael's parents had to agree — noses did run in their family (no pun intended). At 18 months Lisa's interest was in toes. Visitors who came to the house were importuned to remove their shoes, whereupon Lisa solemnly inspected their toes.

Between the ages of two and three children extend their generalizations about the human body. Judging from our conversations with parents, the part of the body most frequently investigated is the genitalia. At an earlier age the children have been interested in their own genitals, but now they are noting the similarities and differences between themselves and other people. Krista commented on her mother's pubic hair. Daryl asked his mother how "she could pee without a ding-dong." Amy was particularly interested in watching her father urinate and was upset she couldn't assume a standing position also. Michael, who seems a bit precocious in this matter, was found one day examining the neighbor boy. Somewhat at a loss for words his mother said, "Why does Lee have his pants down and you don't?" "Doctors don't have their pants down," Michael replied matter of factly.

In discussing visual exploration we have described only a few of the interesting sights that young children notice and comment on. These examples are not meant to suggest that two year old children are supposed to notice such things. Every child sees something different. However, two year olds do have in common certain visual abilities. They can search actively for favorite objects; they are aware of interesting movements and physical transformations going on around them; and they like to match and generalize. The exciting part for parents is to watch what their children see in the world, and to share in the sense of discovery.

Often parents can suggest a new watching activity. Jason was interested in the contrast between light and shadow. One night, after watching slides, his father showed him a shadow game. Holding Jason's teddy bear in front of the light from the projector, a teddy bear shadow appeared on the screen. Jason got the idea and tried casting shadows of his other toys. Jon's mother suggested a light watching activity by giving Jon a flashlight in a dimly lit room. The spot of light was like a live thing, and Jon and his mother enjoyed describing its antics: "It's flying up to the ceiling—Look, the light is jumping on the piano—Oh, it's sleepy, it's lying on the floor."

FILLING AND EMPTYING

Exploring Containers One of the preferred pastimes of toddlers is emptying —bookcases are cleared, milk is poured on the floor, wastebaskets are overturned. Two year olds continue and expand upon this theme. Being taller, stronger, and more agile, they can get into heavy dresser drawers, open closet doors, and climb up to high shelves. As Amy's mother described it, "Amy has graduated to drawers and linen closets." Because of a child's passion for emptying, particular spots in the house may be "out of order" for awhile. Jodi's mother reported that everything had been removed from the lower kitchen cabinets in order to avoid picking up every day. Jed's mother told us the bathroom cabinets were tied up with rope.

In general, however, the emptying behavior of two year olds differs in characteristic ways from that of toddlers. Emptying for its own sake diminishes. Instead emptying is often part of a larger plan. The children are looking for specific objects, and emptying simply represents the fastest way to search. In emptying the cupboards Jodi was looking for the sugar cannister. Amy wanted to find her mother's makeup and jewelry in the dresser drawers.

In many cases emptying serves as a prelude to filling. Most two year olds are engrossed in mastering the skills involved in filling, which usually is more acceptable than emptying. Filling behavior is stimulated by interesting containers. Christopher was not the only child that we observed packing and unpacking an old purse. He talked to himself about his work. "Put it straight—crayons fit—Hope this fits too." Purses have several advantages. They are important adult objects, they are a challenge to open and close, and they can be carried around when full. The world is full of other interesting containers: small suitcases, shopping bags, crayon boxes, plastic bottles, milk cartons, envelopes, etc. New opportunities are discovered all the time. When we visited Timika, for example, we tried to engage her in drawing on a chalkboard. She found it more interesting to work on getting the chalk out of its box.

Benji enjoyed figuring out different combinations of blocks that would fit in his toy trucks. Jodi discovered that four toothbrushes would fit down the drain simultaneously. This kind of experimentation gives children some general notions about volume. One principle they seem to learn is that everything that comes out of a container should fit back in. Usually this can be accomplished after sufficient poking and shoving.

Puzzles

Some containers are puzzles, which means that their contents must be arranged in a precise way. Shape sorters are a very popular kind of puzzle with two year olds. One of Brandon's favorite playthings was a shape sorting toy in the form of a cash register. Brandon never seemed to tire of putting the three different shapes in their respective holes, even though he had memorized the solution long ago. We watched Mary play with a more complicated version—the Tupperware Ball. Not only were there more shapes to recognize but fitting the shapes into the holes required careful orientation. The hexagon piece, for example, would not fit through the hexagon hole unless it was turned in just the right way. Mary had learned to place the piece against the hole and rotate it slowly. Sometimes this strategy worked and sometimes it didn't, but Mary was a patient type and eventually all the pieces were inside.

One shape sorting toy that appeals to every child is a lock and key. Marcie was one of many children in the study who was interested in fitting the key into the front door whenever the family came home. It was as if she was saying, "Let me do the puzzle that opens the house."

Two year olds also are interested in insert puzzles. Heather showed us how she could complete a letter puzzle. Like the shape sorting toys, this puzzle was relatively simple in that each hole could be filled independently. Each piece was a separate puzzle. Single piece puzzles, like Heather's letter puzzle, help children solve the orientation problem. Heather was familiar with the normal orientation of the letters, so she knew how to turn the puzzle pieces in order to make them fit. Heath and Colby, twins who had just turned three, were interested in multi-piece wooden puzzles. Solving this kind of puzzle was considerably more difficult. Each piece that was fit into the puzzle affected the placement of other pieces, and the orientation of the pieces was not always obvious.

There is a dramatic difference between the child who tries to cram a puzzle piece in place and the child who adjusts the position of the piece to match the hole. The first child seems to have no idea why the piece will not fit, while the second child seems to understand spatial relationships automatically. It is like the difference between groping in the dark and walking in the sunlight. Two year old children who have had a chance to play with puzzles are still somewhat in the dark, but the light is dawning. Given a simple enough puzzle, or one with which they are familiar, they rotate the pieces with ease, but given a more difficult or unfamiliar puzzle they go back to random experimentation and brute force.

Obviously puzzles can be frustrating, and parents can play an important role in helping children. Probably the most valuable thing parents can do is to help two year olds pick up their puzzles after playing with them and then put them in a place where they will not be disturbed. We visited several homes in which puzzle pieces were scattered loose in the closet or at the bottom of a toy box. Puzzles were of little use to children in this kind of situation. Helping children to keep the puzzles in order is an excellent way to encourage them to take care of their toys. The advantage of an intact puzzle is self-evident.

Parents also can demonstrate different strategies for solving puzzles. With a child who is just beginning to play with multipiece puzzles, parents can introduce the idea of removing only one or two puzzle pieces at a time and then fitting them back in: "Let's see, I think I'll take out the dog's head and this wheel here. See if you can put them back in.... Now, what do you want to take out?" When all the pieces are removed at once, the problem becomes much more difficult. Parents can help children get started by suggesting they look for a piece with a particular detail or color. Sometimes parents can find the piece and then let the child figure out how it fits in.

What is most striking is the ability of two year old children to memorize puzzle solutions. Even before children can solve the problem of a shape sorting toy, they have memorized what shape goes in what hole. They quickly learn where each piece belongs in an insert puzzle. Completing a multipiece puzzle is primarily a feat of memory. The child has memorized the location of the pieces, the orientation of each piece, and the sequence for putting the pieces in.

Children often demonstrate that they have memorized a puzzle solution by initiating some kind of game. Kelly asked her mother to guess the pictures that were painted under the pieces in the farm puzzle. Kori wanted her mother to become the pupil. "You want to do this one — this one goes here." Erik played a "no" game: Holding a piece that was clearly wrong over a hole in the puzzle he asked, "Think that will fit?"

Nesting toys are a different kind of puzzle. There is a series of boxes, cups, or barrels that fit inside each other. In one way nesting toys are the simplest kind of puzzle, as even the young toddler can manage to fit a little box into a big box. Putting all the pieces together in a nesting toy is a different story. Christopher's play with a set of nesting boxes was typical of two year olds. He enjoyed fitting one box inside another but he was not systematic enough to include all the boxes. The logic of the toy escaped him. If sufficiently interested, two year old children can eventually solve this kind of puzzle through trial and error, and occasionally they may memorize the solution. More often they play with only part of the puzzle.

Michael carried around the red and green barrels from a set of nesting barrels but ignored the others. The green barrel fit inside the red one, and Michael liked to use them to play a stop-light game. Holding up the red barrel, he would say, "It's red — have to stop." His father was supposed to freeze, whether he was walking across the room, chewing food at the table, or putting on his shoes. Then Michael would unscrew the red barrel, remove the green one, and release his motionless father, "O.K. it's green — you can go now."

Pouring and Mixing

Just as a special container stimulates filling and emptying, so does an unusual kind of content. Two year old children enjoy filling a container with small items, such as pieces of macaroni, pennies, shells, pebbles, or buttons. Each child is attracted to different kinds of things. According to his mother, Zacky sometimes spent as long as two hours in the back yard filling a bag with leaves.

By far the most intriguing material, however, is liquid. Here again we see the change in emphasis from experimentation to mastery. Toddlers love to pour out cups of water (milk, juice, or whatever). With two year olds the emphasis is on pouring water into a cup or other container. Lisa, for example no longer poured her milk on the floor. Instead she carefully transferred the milk from one glass to another glass or from a glass to a bowl. Then she proceeded to wash her hands in it. Over and over parents told us about two year olds getting into the refrigerator, and invariably the goal of the children was to pour some liquid refreshment for themselves.

If an adult offered assistance, the children were quite upset. For a two year old, pouring liquid into a glass is both an exciting way to fill a container and an important way of expressing independence.

Another new development is the ability to turn on the faucets. B.J.'s mother enjoyed watching B.J. play in the bathtub. He filled and emptied containers, poured water from one cup to another, drank the bathwater, and splashed vigorously. The situation changed when B.J. learned how to turn on the water. He was constantly at the bathroom sink trying to fill a glass with water, and his mother did not appreciate the pouring and splashing of water all over the floor. She tried to restrict B.J. to one glass of water—when it was time to brush his teeth. However, her attempts were in vain, for B.J. was intent on practicing his new skill.

Once children learn to control faucets, the whole sink or bathtub can become an interesting container. For several months Erik spent his bath time draining the tub and then refilling it. Jodi liked to sneak into the bathroom and fill the sink until it overflowed. Perhaps she did not know how to operate the drain. Then again, she may have seen the whole bathroom as an interesting container to be filled with water.

Filling and emptying containers of water is a theme with many variations. Chad liked to water the plants outside with a hose, filling up the pots with water and watching the water sink out of sight. Erik, who had learned to pour water from a sprinkling can, enjoyed sprinkling his parents when they took a bath. Kori found a unique way to fill a pan with water, squatting in the snow and catching the drops from a melting icicle.

Two years olds play with sand much like they do with water. Containers are filled and then the sand is poured out. A pile of sand may be created, with each new load of poured out sand trickling slowly down the sides. Often the sand that is being scooped up slides off the shovel before it ever reaches a container. Under the tutelage of adults, two year olds learn to pack wet sand in containers and then "pour" out the sand in the form of cakes. In general, however, sand is not used as a medium for construction, but simply as an interesting material for filling and emptying. Mud, snow, and other semi-liquid materials are used for the same purpose.

Sand, mud and snow are also used as containers. Young children like to hide a toy in sand or snow and then retrieve it. Several parents described how their children enjoyed covering their whole bodies in sand. We suspect this variation of filling and emptying does not work as well with snow or mud.

Mixing represents an advanced form of emptying and filling. Two or more materials are poured together into a single container. Two year olds are just beginning to appreciate the possibilities in mixing. They watch with interest as dirt and water are transformed into mud, but soon they are too busy splashing in the mud to investigate the subtleties of mixing. The mixing center par excellence is the kitchen. Heath and Colby argued over whose turn it was to help mix the orange juice. Wendy liked to pour the water into the cookie dough. Jed, contrary to his mother's wishes, enjoyed opening the spices and combining them into rare mixtures.

Drawing and Building

Drawing When we arrived at John's house, his mother told us that John really had a thing about smiley faces. He practiced drawing them on every possible occasion. A little while later we went outside and John quite spontaneously confirmed his mother's statement. He picked up a chunk of limestone from the driveway and used it to draw a perfectly recognizable smiley face in the middle of the sidewalk. As John sat back to admire his product it was obvious that he was not just exploring the properties of the limestone. He was interested in the fact he had created a face.

Sometimes, as with John and his smiley faces, the two year old begins with the notion of drawing a particular object. More frequently the two year old begins by making the drawing and the identification comes next. After scribbling with a blue crayon Jodi looked at her drawing and said, "Look at the blue doggy Jodi made." Often the same object reappears in different scribbles. Nicole saw elephants and triangles; Jamie saw suns and moons; Matthew saw bananas and apples. The tendency to see things in a scribble is encouraged by adults, but it is such a persistent phenomenon that it seems to spring primarily from the perception of the child. Not always, but many times, there is a form in the scribble that suggests the object the child names.

The drawing of most two year olds may lack planning, but it does not lack structure. There are discernable elements in this scribbling. The most common is the circle. Two year olds are strongly committed to making circles. Give them blank paper and you will see large, circular scribbles. There is a smooth rhythm and air of confidence in these circle drawings. Many children also incorporate straight

or jagged lines in their drawings. As Shawn's mother described it, "Shawn has just learned to make bold, definite strokes." Each child acquires some peculiar elements of his own. Erik, for example, put curlicues and banana shapes in many of his scribbles.

The most consistently reported pattern in the drawing of two year olds is a distinction between drawing and writing. There are drawing elements and there are writing elements. Matthew drew either big circles or teeny closed shapes. Lisa created circles or half inch long lines. Shawn made either line scribbles or little chicken scratches. These reports illustrate the fact that many two year olds realize there is a difference between drawing and writing. The children see objects in their drawings, but they see words in their writing. When Krista first made little squiggly marks she said, "This says Krista". She also wrote grocery lists in her hieroglyphics and then read them to her mother. Jennifer, who preferred writing to drawing, insisted on real notebook paper and checks for her scribble words.

Color is an important element of drawing. Usually two year olds use a small number of colors in each drawing, often only one color. Their use of color seems to change as they become more familiar with a particular medium. Children who are just starting to use crayons tend to complete a scribble with one crayon, while those with several months' experience begin to combine colors. When watercolors or tempera paint are first used, the children may go through a period in which a blob of a single color is created. Later on a variety of shapes and colors are more likely. The preferred medium for most children is felt tip pens. Felt tips combine the fine point of a pen for easy scribbling with the vivid color of paints.

It comes as quite a revelation to young children that representational objects can be drawn. Children in our culture are surrounded by pictures, and they learn to recognize pictures at an early age. But it usually is considerably later when they realize pictures can be drawn. Many of the two year olds in our study were so captivated by this discovery that they asked their parents to draw for them. These requests provide an insight into the objects that a particular two year old finds most fascinating. Matthew asked his mother to draw birds, bears, trucks, and trains. Stuart wanted his mother to draw bulldozers. Erik requested chocolate chip cookies and ice cream cones. Some of the children were especially interested in watching letters being printed. Lisa, for example, liked to watch her mother write the names of family members.

Two year olds are also interested in "destroying" a drawing. Andy liked to ask his mother to draw garbage trucks, and then he would color all over the drawing, as if to obliterate it. Erik watched his mother correcting her mistakes by erasing. Sometimes when the drawing was finished, he would say "mistake" and scribble all over it. We watched Chris and Michael, who were twins, as they played with their favorite Christmas toys — two blackboards. They enjoyed scribbling on the boards with chalk, but the highlight of the activity was to make the marks disappear with an eraser. When they tried to share one blackboard a fight broke out over who would get the honor of erasing.

Perhaps the most important thing about the drawing of two year olds is that it is based on discovery. The children are not yet skilled enough to imitate the drawing of others. They discover on their own how to draw circles, how to combine circles, lines and other elements and how to pretend write. They even discover how to hold the crayon. Attempts to teach them the standard way to hold a crayon are not usually successful.

The use of coloring books illustrates our point. Coloring books were present in many of the homes we visited. In fact, we were surprised to find that coloring books were provided more often than blank paper. Almost without exception the two year olds scribbled over the pictures and showed no concern about using the "proper" colors. Even when parents colored with them, the children showed no real interest in completing the printed picture. Their goal seemed to be to create their own picture on top of the printed one. The picture in the book stimulated them to experiment with their own artistic skills.

When children first discover they can create marks, there tends to be an outbreak of scribbling on walls and furniture. Each time a new discovery is made, another burst of intense activity is likely, and the drawing may show up in the wrong place. Darryl's mother was surprised one day to see scribbling on Darryl's bedroom wall — she thought he had finished with that long ago. She was about to scold him when she noticed that the scribbles were a first attempt to write the letters in his name. Lisa, who had given up drawing on walls, discovered she could decorate herself. For several weeks afterwards her arms, legs, and stomach were covered with artwork. These periods of over exuberant drawing usually pass quickly, as the child's desire to explore a new discovery becomes satiated. Sometimes, however, a major confrontation develops over scribbling, and the parents end up taking away all drawing materials until the child is older.

Building As in drawing, the building efforts of the two year old show a distinct developmental progression. The toddler's energy seems to go primarily into knocking down towers that have been built by other people. However, toddlers also are developing important construction skills. They stack objects on top of one another and they lay out toys in a row. In doing so they are learning about two important building principles: balance and straight lines.

Both of these ideas are explored further between two and three. Towers become taller and children discover how to make them both more stable and more pleasing to the eye. One way is to build a tower with objects that are the same size and shape. When Trevor was given a set of blocks with different shapes, he intentionally stacked squares together, circles together, and triangles together, creating columns that were solid and attractive. Younger children sometimes utilize this principle too, but more often their stacking is haphazard.

A second, and more sophisticated, way to design a tower is to place the larger shapes on the bottom and the smaller, less regular shapes on the top. This idea seems patently obvious to us as adults, but children do not learn it for some time. Toddlers

try to balance the most unlikely combinations — a frisbee on top of a toy schoolbus, which is on top of a peanut butter jar. This kind of wild experimentation seems to decline among two year olds. What we observed instead was a beginning interest in balancing smaller objects on top of a larger base. Chris' father had helped him make a block train, and Chris had placed a toy person on top of each car. Ronnie arranged some miniature toys on the top of a bridge constructed by his teacher. Darryl, whose block building was advanced, built some fancy turrets with small, irregular blocks on the top of larger blocks.

Whether the tower of a two year old looks like a smooth column, a delicate turret, or just a random collection, it usually represents something. Towers are incorporated into fantasy play. Often they represent buildings that have some kind of tower on them. Jennifer, for example, considered her towers to be churches and castles. Beverly built a tall tower and described it as the office "where Daddy lives". Although these pretend buildings did not bear much resemblance to their real counterparts, a critical feature had been abstracted and re-created.

Just as towers get taller and lines get longer, they also begin to represent something else. Matthew lines up all his toy animals on the back of the sofa and called it a bridge. Colby made long lines of blocks and referred to them as trains. Michael put his Fisher Price people in a row and pretended it was a parade. As these examples illustrate, two year olds are not limited to building lines with blocks. A line can be created with puzzle pieces, silverware, or beads on a string.

Sooner or later the two year old who is interested in building lines makes a major discovery — the corner. Terry learned how to make a T with just two blocks and then proceeded to make more elaborate T's with many blocks. Erik changed a block train into an airplane by adding stubby wings. Matthew created an irregular ring of blocks that represented the record store where he recently had got a new record.

When children show an interest in creating flat designs, parents can help maintain or extend this interest. With just a few suggestions or demonstrations the child who has learned to make T's and turn corners can make fences, booths, stalls, beds, playgrounds, or perhaps a swimming pool. Small flat blocks of different shapes encourage representational designs, while uniform size cubes are particularly good for line explorations.

Traditional construction toys, such as tinker toys and Lincoln Logs, were designed for children older than three. They require more coordination and dexterity than two year olds possess. However, the tinker toy idea, fitting a peg in a hole, does appeal to two year old children, and there are versions that are satisfactory. Certain pegboards are appropriate, and stringing beads can be used with dowel rods. Plastic blocks and rods that are larger than the usual tinker toys also are available. Although the possibilities for construction are more limited with these toys than with blocks, similar kinds of linear experiments take place.

The most popular construction toys are the type that consist of interlocking blocks. There are oversize versions of these toys that are suitable for two year olds. We watched Robert and his father build a Lego train during our visit. Again, this type of toy is less flexible than a set of blocks, but it may give the child a feeling of having built something more substantial. With construction toys two year old children seem to be primarily interested in learning how to connect the pieces, and less attention is paid to experimenting with different forms.

Arts and Crafts

Arts and crafts projects represent a kind of activity midway between drawing and building. They combine the fluidity of drawing with the three dimensional quality of building. In general arts and crafts are beyond the capacities of a two year old. Beverly's mother regularly helped her do arts and crafts projects from a Sesame Street magazine, but she began to sense that Beverly was being pushed too hard. Beverly started to complain "I can't" whenever her mother suggested that she play with blocks and crayons. Lisa's mother also encouraged cutting and pasting projects but the activities were carefully planned to include both Lisa and her four year old brother. In contrast to drawing and building, arts and crafts projects require close supervision at this age and are most effective when older children are included. Even so, the focus of the two year old is on manipulating the material more than creating a product.

Playing with clay is a good example. Two year old children occasionally create a product with clay, such as a cake, a hamburger, or a snake. They are most likely to do so when imitating older children who are playing with them. For the most part they enjoy pounding, squeezing, and poking the clay, and if left alone they invariably end up tearing the clay into little pieces and throwing it around the room. Then the only end product is a mess to be cleaned up. Many of the families we visited were not enthusiastic about letting their two year olds play with clay or playdough. Apparently the parents thought the inconvenience outweighed the possible benefits.

Most two year olds do not have the skill to use paper as a medium for craft projects either. If they can use scissors at all, it is simply to cut a large piece of paper into smaller pieces. Smearing glue around is fun for a few minute, but most of it ends up in the wrong place and the children get discouraged.

We did notice that two year old children created their own version of cutting and pasting. For example, eating toast became a craft project for Matthew. He "cut" the material by taking a bite of toast. Then he looked at the remaining bread to see what it resembled. Michael saw letters and numbers in half

eaten pretzels. Examples of "pasting" projects were even more common. Erik stuck a dozen pieces of scotch tape on his broken firehat. Jodi sneaked into the bathroom and covered herself with bandaids. Amy stuck pencils into a ball of clay. Brian planted twigs in the dirt.

These examples are typical of the two year old's orientation. The emphasis is on manipulation, on the process of tearing apart or sticking together. Occasionally a product may result, but it is more of a coincidence than a planned outcome.

Finding Out How Things Work

In a sense all exploration involves how things work. The child who watches water going down a drain is learning something about how things work, as is the child who tries to build a tower. However, in this section we want to concentrate on activities in which children focus on mechanical relationships and the process of cause and effect. We will look at situations where the children want to turn on a machine or use a tool, where they want to make something dramatic happen or see how something is put together.

Machines The pre-eminent machine in our culture is the automobile. From an early age children want to operate this machine. The aspect of driving that most stands out in their minds is turning the steering wheel. Two year olds continue to play with the steering wheel, but they also expand their repertoire of driving skills. They learn to insert the ignition key, honk the horn, turn on the accessories, or even step on the gas and make the engine roar. But steering still stands out. Two year old children want to steer all kinds of vehicles, the tractor lawn mower in a department store, the bulldozer sitting idle in the vacant lot next door, the neighbor's motorcycle. Marcie, for example, was trying to steer her uncle's new car. She voiced the sentiment of a lot of two year olds when she said, "This car is mine".

Two year olds are likely to be fascinated by car junkyards, if they have the chance to see one. Benjie and Jamie, two brothers we visited, had an ideal situation from this standpoint. Their father, who salvaged parts off of old vehicles, had over a dozen cars and boats parked around the house. There was no problem sharing. While Jamie steered a grounded motorboat, Benjie drove an old Volkswagen. It was a two year old's dream come true.

Most of the exciting machines in a child's environment are electrical. The television is a case in point. With the push of a button the dark screen is transformed into a talking picture. Many of the two year olds we visited were discouraged from touching

the television at all, but still most of them had learned how to turn the set on and off. They wanted to practice this skill, which led to trouble with their parents. In general the children had learned surprisingly little about how to operate a television. They seemed unaware of most of the controls and rarely tried to change the channel, adjust the color, or raise the volume, even when their parents were not looking.

Stereos present a similar situation. Two year olds usually are trained to stay away from them and do not know much about operating them. Telephones are a bit more accessible. Like B. J. many two year olds have mastered the art of dialing, and it is only a matter of time before they make a connection with a distant party. B. J.'s telephone was also installed on a jack, which he soon learned how to unplug. When he wasn't dialing for strangers, he was carrying around a disconnected phone. The push button telephone, which is becoming common, is even more fun for children because each number emits a distinct tone when pressed.

The list of machines that a two year old may get interested in goes on and on. Parents told us of children wanting to operate slide projectors, hair dryers, blenders, lawn mowers, garage door openers, electric typewriters, sewing machines, and power drills. Frequently these machines are either too dangerous or too valuable for children to explore, and a power struggle ensues. In Brian's case the confrontation was especially severe. He was not allowed in one room of the house because it was an office. However, he continued to sneak in the office. His mother would find him pulling and twisting the parts of the typewriter, as if he were trying to dismantle it. Probably he simply was trying to turn it on. It was an electric typewriter and he was looking for the switch that made it work.

Two year old children are attracted to machines because they are important, adult objects. Operating a machine is not only an adult privilege; it often is a way of expressing adult-like power. Chopping food in the blender, or opening the heavy garage door, is an impressive act. It makes the children feel they have caused a powerful change. The children want to understand how the machines work, but only in a practical sense. They want to turn them on, to make something exciting happen. Eventually the thrill of operating a particular machine passes, at least until a new way of manipulating it is discovered. The two year old who wants to practice turning the television off and on will have no interest in doing so as a four year old. Instead the four year old may enjoy flipping the channel selector or adjusting the antenna.

In deciding how to handle the desire of two year olds to operate machines, this practical orientation should be kept in mind. On the one hand, no great intellectual damage will result if children are forbidden to touch the television or stereo. They would not be learning much about electricity in any case. On the other hand, if children are allowed to operate a machine, they may soon master the process and grow tired of it. Instead of dragging on for months, or even years, the conflict over a particular machine may be dissipated in a short time.

Each situation is different. Sometimes parents can supervise children while they explore a machine. Colby and Heath were allowed to use the garage door opener under supervision. Erik could operate the slide projector as long as his father gave him guidance. In some cases young children get so proficient that they are able to operate a machine without assistance. B. J. could be trusted with the hair dryer; Jed handled the vacuum cleaner by himself.

With electrical machines there still is the problem of plugging the equipment in. Nearly all of the children in our study were interested in putting plugs into wall outlets, and nearly all parents did not think the children were old enough to learn this skill. Although some of the children accepted their parents' admonitions, others paid no attention. Putting covers on the outlets did not help because the children were old enough to pry them off.

When children insist on acquiring this skill, despite warnings, threats, and spankings, it seems advisable to help them learn. Mary's parents had taught her the first step in learning how to handle plugs—taking a plug out. She was allowed to unplug cords, but not to plug them back in. So far this compromise had worked, although Mary was just two years old. Shawn's parents had gone a step further. They finally had agreed to let Shawn put plugs in the outlet while they were watching. Nothing had discouraged him from trying on his own, including several shocks. In fact Shawn was so intrigued by electricity that a favorite comment was, "Let's talk about plugs." Then he would point out different kinds of plugs in the house and expect his mother to elaborate on this engrossing subject.

Sometimes children are satisfied with the appearance of operating a machine. B.J. was not allowed to plug in the hair dryer, but he did not care. He stuck the cord behind the refrigerator and was quite pleased with this approximation. Mary was content to play with an extra telephone that was left unplugged. It never rang and had no dial tone, but that did not bother her.

Children also adopt secondary roles when denied a primary role in operating a machine. Most of the time they cannot operate the steering wheel of the family car, but they can assume other roles. Lisa unbuckled her seat belt every time the car stopped, at a traffic light, at the drive-up bank, at a toll booth. Naturally she did not like to be restrained, yet there was more than a dislike of restraint in her behavior. As soon as the car started again, she wanted to fasten her seat belt, much to the frustration of her mother. Controlling the seat belt was Lisa's way of participating in the operation of the car. Angie, who was always asking if she could steer the car, settled for opening the car door by herself. Jason took charge of pushing down the lock buttons on all the doors.

Mechanical Toys

The major way we handle the desire of two year olds to operate machines is to give them toy substitutes. Nearly every two year old has a toy telephone to compensate for not being allowed to play with the real one. We give the young children toy radios, cameras, record players, and even televisions. From an adult viewpoint these substitutes are often rather pathetic as machines, but most two year olds seem happy as long as a toy telephone makes a little jingle, or a toy radio plays a simple tune.

The children are more interested in operating the toys than in the quality of the outcome. When we visited Laura, she showed us her record player. As soon as one record began, she stopped it and turned it over, or else put on another record. Manipulating the record player was more fun than listening to the music. The same thing happened with the viewmaster. The excitement lay in putting the discs in the machine and pressing the advance mechanism. The pictures themselves drew only a passing glance.

We do not need to describe in detail the enormous amount of time that young children spend driving toy cars instead of real ones. Steering wheel toys are particularly popular amoung two year olds. John was one of several children who were very attached to this kind of toy. With nothing but a plastic steering wheel and a plastic C.B. radio, John was ready to roll. Amy, who did not have such a toy, invented her own steering wheel by turning a swivel chair upside down.

Two year old children are interested in a variety of other mechanical toys. We noticed several children who had renewed their interest in the Jack-in-the-Box toy that they had received as a baby. Now they could operate the toy, push the clown down inside, close the lid, and turn the crank. In a similar way we saw children winding up musical, stuffed animals that had been with them since infancy. Busyboxes were once again appealing because this time the child could easily manipulate the mechanisms and study the cause and effect relationships. There were new mechanical toys as well. Wind-up vehicles could be activated. Toys that worked according to air pressure could be made to jump. Spring loaded toys could be operated successfully. These mechanical toys stimulate the same pattern of behavior as adult machines. An intense burst of interest is likely as the child seems to master the skill involved in making the toy work. Once this skill is developed, and the child has practiced it sufficiently, the toy loses its appeal and starts to gather dust.

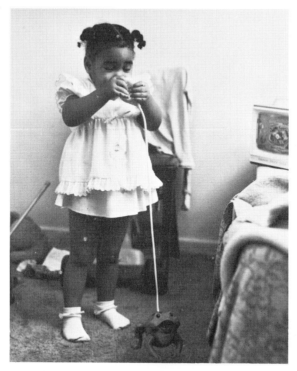

Tools

Two year old children are interested in tools for much the same reasons as machines. Tools are associated with adults and they can be used to make something happen. In fact tools are a kind of machine and many modern tools are electrical. But even the traditional, non-electrical tools are favorites with two year old children. They try to mop the floor, rake the yard, sweep the steps, and dig a hole in the garden. Once again, manipulating the tool is more important than the quality of the outcome.

The children also are attracted to the class of tools that are used to make or fix things. Between the ages of two and three many children are allowed to handle hammers, screwdrivers, and wrenches. Although toy tools are available, real ones are often easier to use. The children are most successful at hammering. Benjie and Jamie helped their father hammer out pieces of copper tubing from old air conditioners. Each boy had his own hammer and could spend as long as he liked pounding on the tubing. Screwdrivers and wrenches are often used like hammers, to tap and poke at things. Matthew always wanted to help his father work on the car, but scratching the paint with a screwdriver was not what his father had in mind. This kind of tool play is more acceptable when working on a tricycle or a Big Wheel.

Some children are unusually skilled with tools. We watched Frank, who was three years old, drive a nail, try to cut a wire with a set of pliers, and start to pry off a hubcap with a screwdriver. His mother described how Frank always took things apart. He removed the cork seals from around the windows. His favorite toy was a truck that could be reduced to pieces. He crushed his food to bits at the table. In fact one of the most exciting experiences of his life had been helping his grandfather take the dishwasher apart.

The outstanding function of many tools is to take things apart, and this is the characteristic that children sieze on. Children like Frank, who are especially interested in mechanical relationships, will be more destructive. Shawn, for example, went beyond most children in investigating how the toilet worked. Not content to just learn how the toilet was flushed, he kept removing the back and tinkering with the mechanism inside. When a child shows a strong inclination to take things apart, one idea is to provide an "explorer" box full of objects that can be dismantled. Of course someone has to put them back together if they are to be used again.

Even children who are not proficient with tools are interested in the process of taking things apart. Heather was adept at peeling a tangerine. Angela enjoyed unsnapping clothes and unzipping zippers. Mary kept breaking off the figurines in a shadow box and asking her mother to glue them back. She was not the only child we saw who played the game of "I break it — you fix it."

Finally, there is a class of tools with the special function of making music. This possibility interests two year olds but typically requires too much skill. At some point or other many of the children had learned to bang on a drum, strike a xylophone, or plunk a piano. Some of the children had learned to play a simple wind instrument, such as a harmonica. However, going from sound experimentation to playing music is a big leap. Darryl, a three year old, was the only child we observed trying to sound out a tune. His grandfather was very interested in music, and Darryl tried to imitate him when he played songs on Darryl's xylophone. Darryl's grandfather also had taught him to keep the beat on a drum when they were singing. In general, the two year olds in our study were more involved in learning to move their bodies in time to music than in playing musical instruments.

Moving Through Space

Explorations

With Movement Exploration is active: it involves movement. We already have described some of the ways two year olds move objects as they explore them. Puzzle pieces are rotated until they fit, blocks are arranged to make an enclosure, a hammer is swung against a wooden peg. These are movements on a relatively small scale.

Movement on a larger scale is more characteristic of two year olds. Even when they are exploring a puzzle, a set of blocks, or a toy workbench, they are up and down, circling around—now squatting now standing, now running to the window. Movements of the whole body represent an important part of exploration. The children are discovering the possibilities and limitations of their own bodies, and at the same time they are learning about the space that surrounds them.

Toddlers are interested in testing themselves against large and cumbersome objects. They strain to push, pull, and lift these obstacles. Two year olds continue this kind of body exploration, although their interest seems to be waning somewhat. The most common example we found on our visits was trying to open a heavy door, such as the front door or the car door.

The primary mode of the active two year old is not pushing or carrying, but running. Children at this age are inveterate runners. They are willing to run even when they are too tired to walk. However, the racing technique of older children has not been mastered yet. Although the children run with gusto, their short, choppy steps go nowhere fast. And trying to turn a sharp corner often results in an abrupt, and painful, landing.

Running and jumping go together. The young of many species are noted for their playful cavorting. Between two and three years of age children learn to put a little hop, skip, or jump into their running. When we say "little," we do not exaggerate. Running and jumping over a sock, or over the hose, is considered quite an accomplishment.

Jumping with the aid of a spring is a different matter. Heather demonstrated for us the typical exuberance with which a two year old rides a rocking horse. The higher the bounce the better the ride. These kind of creatures are available in many parks, and children can be observed wrenching them this way and that, trying to get as much spring as possible. For those who do not have an exotic beast at hand, there always is a bed that can be jumped on. Two year old children have so much fun learning to jump that many parents allow a limited amount of this jumping, at least until the children get bigger and heavier.

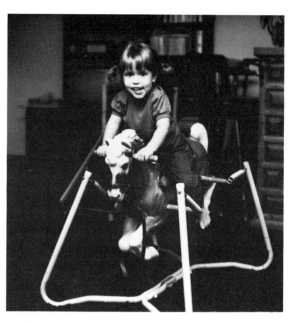

Jumping down is another popular pastime. Two year old children do not have enough strength to jump up very fast, but they do have the nerve to jump down, especially if a soft landing is provided for them. We watched Chris and Michael jumping off a coffee table onto a cushion on the floor. The first jump was approached with trepidation, but after that they jumped with the abandon of experienced paratroopers. Jumping down could be described as controlled falling. The end result is the same as falling, but being in control makes the experience pleasant.

Two year olds continue to develop their climbing skills but there are large differences between individual children. Some children become fearful of heights, while others demonstrate a new strength and agility in their climbing. Brian showed us how he climbed up on the bar to watch the fish. Benjie climbed on the roof of a car. Matthew was one of several children who enjoyed climbing in and out of a crib. Climbing outside was more difficult. The bars on jungle gyms seemed too far apart for most two year olds and the drop to the bottom too great a fall. Jason, who was a talented climber, was willing to try a jungle gym only when his mother was nearby to catch him. Climbing in a tree presented similar difficulties. Matthew enjoyed the view but getting up and down required help. Climbing a ladder on a slide or scaling a chain link fence, were more satisfactory challenges for the two year olds we visited.

Throwing is a body movement that often develops dramatically between two and three. Toddlers flip objects more than they throw them. They do not get their bodies behind the throw and there is only a slight ability to aim. The object may be released too early and fall behind the child. If not, it is likely to go flying off at almost any angle. By the age of three, however, children can aim their throws, although they may choose to tease an adult by throwing a ball in the wrong direction. Because of their greater ability to throw, two year olds like to play with small balls that can be grasped in one hand. This is in contrast to the preference of toddlers for large balls that can be lugged around.

Small balls are for throwing, large ones are for catching. Billy was able to catch a volleyball by trapping it against his body. This ability was decidedly limited though. The ball had to be thrown from a very short distance and it had to hit Billy squarely in the chest. Suzanne, on the other hand, was able to catch a large balloon with just her hands. The balloon traveled through the air so slowly that she could track its motion and respond accordingly.

Balls can be rolled along the ground as well as thrown through the air. Two year olds enjoy a game of catch in which a ball is rolled back and forth. In contrast to the toddler who squats down to catch a ball just as it goes past him, a two year old anticipates the path of the ball and gets his body in the proper position ahead of time. Toy cars are also used for rolling games in which the children experiment with propulsion. John showed us how he could send a new race car speeding across the room with a single thrust.

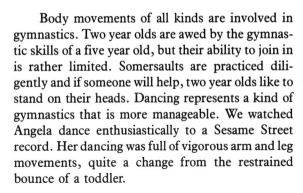

Body movements of all kinds are involved in gymnastics. Two year olds are awed by the gymnastic skills of a five year old, but their ability to join in is rather limited. Somersaults are practiced diligently and if someone will help, two year olds like to stand on their heads. Dancing represents a kind of gymnastics that is more manageable. We watched Angela dance enthusiastically to a Sesame Street record. Her dancing was full of vigorous arm and leg movements, quite a change from the restrained bounce of a toddler.

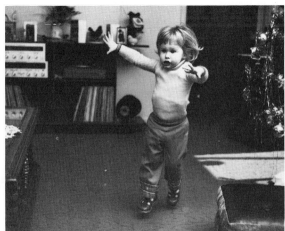

The arm and leg coordination that enables two year olds to run and jump and dance can be applied to a tricycle. Wheels can replace feet as a means of transportation. This is not an instantaneous process however. The children do not realize the initial force that is necessary to overcome inertia, and they are not sure when each foot should be pressed down on the pedal.

The first movements are a matter in inches, and, as Jason demonstrated to us, they are just as likely to be in a backward as a forward direction.

The best practicing surface is one that slopes very slightly down hill. Too steep a downgrade may lead to catastrophe, but the smallest incline will stop a novice cyclist in his tracks. Just like a motorist out of gas, the two year old who gets too frustrated by the whole process can get off and push. In fact some children get so good at pushing and steering simultaneously that they are somewhat late to try riding. Then one day they begin to pedal, and in a short time they are riding as if they had been doing it all their lives.

A similar kind of coordination is involved in pumping a swing, but it is harder to learn. At least most children take longer to learn it. Perhaps it is because parents are more willing to push a swing than a tricycle. Wherever two year olds are gathered, it is almost a certainty that sooner or later they will be found sitting in swings, being pushed by an older person. Swinging is a relaxing activity that children and parents share at this age — a time for talking and laughing together. At some point in the future the parents will expect their children to do the work themselves, but for the time being they are happy to play the servant's role.

Playgrounds in general are a happy place for two year olds and their parents. Most of the children have overcome earlier fears of slides or swings. Yet they are not quite ready to join in the rough and tumble play of older children. Parents do not have to stand over the children in fear that they are going to break their necks, but at the same time they are still needed by the child — to push the merry-go-round gently, to catch the child at the bottom of a tall slide, to help the child get down from a platform he has climbed onto. It is a situation in which parents can both relax and participate.

Action Games

There are other ways that parents and two year olds share physical activity. Jon initiated wrestling matches by jumping on his father whenever he lay down. When Shawn's mother propped her legs on the coffee table, Shawn used them like a bar for somersaulting to the floor. Jenny and her mother liked to put on a record and intersperse their housework with dancing. This is the most interesting characteristic of physical exploration — it invariably leads to a shared activity.

These shared activities have the qualities of a game. There are no winners or losers, but certain, unwritten rules define the role each player will take. The rules insure that the game will unfold in a similar way every time it is played. Running leads to chase games. Actually chase games start as soon as children can crawl. By the time children are two years old chasing may have evolved into a simple version of hide and seek. The children run away and hide, knowing full well that their parents will find them because they always hide in the same places. Timika liked to hide behind the curtain. Angie climbed into the fireplace. Any place that a two year old can just squeeze into is a good spot — an old box, the dirty clothes basket, between the bed and the wall. Chase games may be elaborated verbally. Jason's father sang 'All Around the Mulberry Bush' as he chased Jason. The words were adapted to fit the situation: "All around the living room, the Daddy chased Jason; Jason sat down in a chair, and the Daddy sat down on him."

Jumping leads to jumping games. Usually the child is the jumper and the parent is the catcher. Whenever Robert saw his father was close enough, he jumped off the bathtub ledge or off the crib railing. There wasn't much his father could do but catch Robert, and so far, his father told us, he had not missed. We suspected he enjoyed catching Robert. Erik requested a jumping game while shopping. Each parent held one of his hands while saying, "Jack be nimble, Jack be quick, Jack jump over the candlestick." On the word "over" Erik jumped as high as he could. At the same time his parents lifted him, and he seemed to jump two or three feet in the air.

Throwing also leads to games of catch. A favorite version among two year olds was demonstrated by Robert. Before going to sleep he threw all his stuffed animals out of the crib, while his father tried to catch them. Perhaps his father threw them back in the next morning — we did not stay around for that part of the game. For Jason and his mother the bathtub offered a good spot for a game of catch.

She threw a rubber ball to Jason while he was in the tub. He missed the ball but it was floating right next to him and was easy to retrieve. Jason flung the wet ball back to his mother, who threw him a high one that made a big splash as it landed.

Running, jumping and throwing — these are the activities that seem to stimulate the greatest number of parent-child play routines. However, we observed other examples. In Matthew's home wrestling had led to a pretend boxing game. Riding a tricycle became a game for Laura when she rode through a tunnel formed by her father's legs. Robert and his parents played a dancing game called "circle" when one of his favorite records was put on the phonograph. Every form of physical activity has the potential of becoming a shared game.

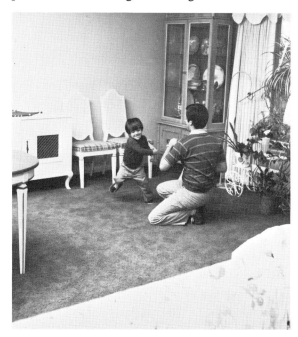

One reason games occur in connection with physical activity is that both children and parents think it is important to develop physical skill. Parents enjoy teaching children how to use their bodies, and they take a great deal of pride in the growing physical ability of their children. This feeling of pride is reflected by the children. Brandon showed us how he could do a somersault. Jodi was proud of being able to stand up in a swing. Daniel was able to jump in a pool and swim back to the side. As he put it, "I make it." Swimming is particularly prominent in Florida, but we imagine the same kind of excitement surrounds skiing and ice skating in other parts of the country.

Going Places

As children move their bodies they learn about the properties of the space around them. Distance takes on more meanig as it comes to be measured in terms of how far one has run, or jumped, or thrown a ball. Relative position becomes understood more fully as children move in, out, over, under, and through other objects.

Most interesting, however, is a two year old's growing awareness of the way space is organized. Beverly's mother was amazed that Beverly recognized the outside of the hairdresser's shop several months after their visit. This kind of memory for places is surprising, but it is typical of two year olds. Children learn to recognize special buildings (like the doctor's office), landmarks, or even whole neighborhoods very quickly. Between the ages of two and three they begin to remember the routes that link these familiar places. Beverly's mother discovered that Beverly liked to direct her driving. Beverly would point in the direction the car should go, and more often than not, they would end up at the right place, grandmother's house, the grocery store, the beach, etc.

A more intense kind of exploration occurs when two year old children investigate the spatial layout of their immediate environment. They have long been familiar with the organization of their own home, although some new places may be discovered, like the back of a clothes closet or the space behind the furnace. The space right outside the house is more of an unknown quantity. Two year olds who are lucky enough to have a fenced-in yard can go out and explore this territory at their leisure. They can closely scrutinize such details as the mud puddle under the drainpipe, the pile of bricks under the apple tree, and the garbage can near the fence. Two years old is a good time for really getting to know the back yard, and as Shawn's mother pointed out, it can have a calming influence. Shawn was less restless inside the house after they moved to a new house with a yard.

Whether or not two year old children have a yard, many of them get a strong urge to wander farther. We watched Kim scale a five foot fence in order to chase a duck. Benjie and Jamie liked to visit the neighbor next door (although her cat did not like to visit their dog). Brian had visited the lady across the back fence and now was starting to go down the block. It seems especially nice for two year olds to have this kind of relationship with neighbors. However, most of the parents in our study were concerned about their children wandering alone at this age. There were dangers the children did not appreciate, and there was the possibility of getting lost. Compromises were common. Children were allowed to ride their tricycles along the sidewalk in front of the house, but no further. Or they could go to the corner, but no further. They could visit the next door neighbor, but no further. And so forth.

By far the most satisfactory compromise, from a child's point of view, is when parents agree to accompany a child as he wanders. We wandered along with B. J. and his mother on a walk around the block. During the walk B. J. was constantly exploring. Some of the things he found interesting were things that appeal to adults too. He stopped to pet a neighbor's dog, picked some wildflowers, and rolled a few smooth stones around in his hand. Other things B. J. stopped for showed the special worldview of a two year old. At one point he circled a big tree, and at another point he tried climbing a fire hydrant. The walk had no definite destination and was not confined to the sidewalk. B. J. strayed onto lawns and walked along ledges. His mother stayed nearby, reminding him of dangers, talking about the sights, and lending a helping hand when necessary. On the way back he needed even more than a helping hand, so his mother gave him a piggy back ride the rest of the way.

Exporing space is a leisurely process for two year old children. B. J.'s walk was a success because he set the pace. Other families have described to us how unsuccessful walks can be when parents set the goals. Matthew's father was looking forward to hiking during a family vacation to the mountains, but the vacation was a disaster. Matthew was not interested in keeping a steady pace in order to reach some distant spot of beauty. Why should he press on to see some waterfall when he could throw twigs and rocks into the little stream flowing next to the path. Hiking became a hassle. The best part of the vacation, according to Matthew's father, was wandering around every evening looking for firewood and then building a campfire. That was the kind of hiking that made sense to Matthew.

Watching B.J. on his walk, we saw a kind of playful experimentation. With each new object B.J. seemed to be wondering — what can I do to this, what can this do to me. We have emphasized in this chapter the two year old's desire to master skills through exploration, but children at this age are still expert experimenters, especially when exploring something new. They twist and pull, poke and tap, drop and throw, and even taste objects, just to see what will happen.

For many two year olds the outdoors represents a new and exciting environment for experimentation. Stores, especially large department stores, offer similar possibilities. No longer so overwhelmed by the hustle and bustle of shoppers or by the staggering array of merchandise, two year old children become more active in stores. They play with items on the shelves, hide under the clothes racks, and wander into the changing rooms. The children are interested in learning the layout of the store. In their independent jaunts they venture further and further from parents and may set off intentionally to investigate another department.

Again, this kind of exploration can be enjoyable for both parents and children if there is plenty of time, enough time to talk to children about what they are discovering and to discuss the limitations of exploration in a store. Playing with a three panel mirror or riding the escalator may be the highlight of the day. Unfortunately, shopping often is a hurried project in which the child's instinct for exploration must be subordinated to the parent's need to get finished quickly.

Summary So far in our discussions of explorations we have focused on daily living experiences. As we talked with parents about the high points of living with a two year old, over and again parents described how marvelous it was to share their child's delight with a new experience or discovery.

Jenny's mother described the first time the family went trick or treating on Halloween.

"Jenny was dressed as Raggedy Ann and we both loved making up her face. At first she didn't know what to do but after the first few houses, she was walking right up to the door herself saying, 'trick or treat' and opening her bag. She still talks about it."

Benji's family listed as high point an evening at the races when Benji sat in a stock car. Allison's family talked about going to a nearby pond and watching Allison feed the ducks.

In almost every case outstanding moments that parents described were not elaborate events. Most two year olds are not ready for large scale sightseeing excursions. The two year old needs to set his own pace and determine his own interests. Parents should not be disappointed if the highlight of the circus for the two year old is a balloon that stays up in the air or the highlight of a football game is going under the turnstile.

In this chapter we have emphasized five different kinds of explorations. They have been discussed separately, but in reality they occur together much of the time. Being able to manipulate the water faucet encourages children to explore filling, yet turning on the water faucet is also a way of operating a machine, and watching the water disappear down the drain is a form of visual exploration. Building a pen for a set of zoo animals involves both constructing and filling, and probably the animals will jump out of the pen sooner or later and start moving through space.

The objects that give rise to the most exploration are those that lend themselves to different kinds of exploration. Cars and other vehicles, for example, stimulate a great variety of exploration. Riding in a car is one of the most interesting ways to explore things visually. Cars are exciting machines with many different parts to be operated. As the car moves from place to place it enables a child to organize space into a set of familiar routes. Cars, and especially trucks, are containers, and though children do not often have the opportunity to fill real vehicles, filling toy cars and trucks is a common form of play.

Through exploration young children develop skill in using their bodies, but they also gain a greater understanding of the world they live in.

They learn about the nature of various materials and objects, now they can be combined, taken apart, or restructured into new forms. Above and beyond this information about specific objects, the children develop some broad principals for organizing the world. Most two year olds in our culture live in an urban environment and so their organizing concepts are related to the idea of a city.

First, there is the notion of work done outside the home. The children realize that one or both parents go to a certain place and work. The nature of the work may be a mystery, but many two year olds are aware that money is associated with work. They also begin to see that different people perform different kinds of work. Two year olds especially notice the workers with uniforms or special hats: policemen, bus drivers, garbage men, barbers, construction workers.

A second idea involves buying and selling. Most prominent is the fact that food is bought at a grocery store. Children also learn at an early age that gas is bought at a service station. Gradually this idea expands, as the children begin to distinguish the separate functions of drug stores, hardware stores, toy stores, etc. Some department stores have just about everything, while other stores have only one kind of thing.

A third concept is the idea of private ownership. Almost everything belongs to someone, and this is a hard lesson to learn. The things in stores belong to the store until they are bought. The cars in the street belong to different people and cannot be entered at will. Even the grass along the sidewalk is the property of someone else and must be trod on carefully.

These ideas, and others like them, are not generated by any one kind of experience. They are the cumulative result of exploration of all kinds. Between the ages of two and three these ideas are still vague, and they are not connected into any consistent system of thought. They are significant though, because they indicate that the children are becoming aware of the economic and technological structure of our culture. The city is becoming a natural and predictable environment in their eyes.

The importance of parents in guiding and fostering exploration has been implicit throughout this chapter. Although two year old children try to conduct some of their exploration in secret, they typically want parents to pay attention to their activity and to talk with them about it. It is even better if the parents participate in the exploration too. As Christopher's father told us, "Chris is happy to play with his toys as long as I play along, but if I don't pay attention to him he will tear the place up."

Being involved with children as they explore gives parents a chance to warn children of dangers and to explain restrictions. It also gives parents the opportunity to introduce new ideas. Exploration is not always a discovery experience. Parents can suggest a strategy for completing a puzzle, demonstrate a new way of building, or invent an action game. As long as they are not made to feel inferior, two year old children are eager for new ideas.

Every new idea, whether it originates with parents or children, is potentially frustrating. Parents who are avid explorers themselves need to guard against leading their children into activities that are likely to be frustrating. At the same time parents can help children deal with frustration. Mary's mother was particularly sensitive in this way. When Mary had trouble blowing soap bubbles, her mother tried also and intentionally failed. The natural inclination would have been to try demonstrating to Mary the proper technique. However, in this case Mary's mother judged it more important to support Mary's feelings by modeling failure. Sometimes parents can help make failure humorous by joking about the puzzle piece that is upside down or the block tower that has collapsed. Verbal formulas can be offered for easing the pain of failure — "That's a hard one," "This puzzle is tricky."

Finally parents can go along with the desire of children to repeat and practice their new found skills. Two year old children complete a favorite puzzle over and over, build the same kind of block structure again and again, play with the same tools, etc. Many of these routines need parent participation. Earlier we emphasized the kind of interaction games that develop around running, jumping, and throwing, but parent-child games become associated with all forms of exploration. Exploration is concerned only partially with the new and the exciting. The ultimate goal of exploration is mastery, and children look to their parents to help them reach this goal.

Chapter II—Imagination

Developmental Advances	33
Individual Differences	35
The Actor Style	36
Producer–Director Style	45
Reasons for Pretending	48
Making Sense Out of the World	48
Compensating for Feelings of Inadequacy	49
Ways to Foster Imaginative Play	52
The Role of the Adult	52
The Props	56
Things To Put On	56
Things To Travel On	56
Places To Go To	57
Things To Carry	57
Things To Use	57
Playscapes	58
Miniature Type Props	58
Raw Materials	58
Play Space	59
Summary	59

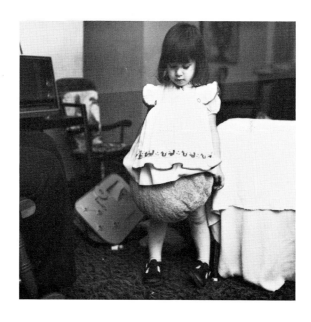

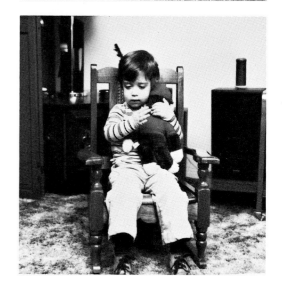

Chapter II
Imagination

"Picnic's ready," Melinda announces. "Everybody sit down. No, Big Bird, you sit up over here and don't fall down."

As we watch Melinda arranging her Sesame Street characters around the picnic table, we get the feeling that we have just walked into the middle of an elaborate stage production. Melinda is a rather bossy director instructing the various characters as to how they should play their parts.

"Want a hamburger, Big Bird?" Melinda asks as she shoves a red poker chip into Big Bird's beak. "Yes, I want a hamburger." Big Bird answers in a high squeaky voice. "So do I," answers Melinda as she pours some imaginary ketchup onto a stack of poker chips. As Melinda pretends to bite into her poker chip sandwich, it appears that she has shifted her role from director to actor. Then, suddenly she is back to being director. "Up, up everybody. Hurry, hurry. Picnic's over, rain is coming down!"

Although adults may do their own kind of pretending, just pretend play is the special trademark of childhood. Whether the youngster is surrounded by a roomful of Fisher Price miniatures, or out in a backyard with nothing but a clothespin, the child's imagination creates its special alchemy. The Fisher Price characters walk and talk and the old-fashioned clothespin becomes a soldier, an airplane, or a fishing rod.

In this chapter we are planning to look at imaginative play from several points of view:
1. What are the major developmental advances in imaginative play between two and three years old?
2. How can we describe individual differences in imaginative play behavior?
3. What purpose does imaginative play serve?
4. How can we foster imaginative play?

DEVELOPMENTAL ADVANCES

In a sense two years old is a transition period for the development of imaginative play. Toddlers are more apt to be imitators than pretenders. As they jabber into a toy telephone or sweep the floor with an over-sized broom, they are copying, as accurately as they can, a performance they have witnessed. But as they approach two years old, we begin to see subtle changes in their style of playing. Play episodes are extended over a longer time frame. Repetitive imitation decreases and play themes begin to emerge. Props are used more extensively, and the same props are used in a variety of ways. Favorite themes are revised and expanded, and new themes are introduced. Finally and most important, children use language to describe and elaborate their just pretend themes.

Let's take a closer look at how the developmental changes in imaginative play come about. As young as two years old, when she had just about mastered the two word phrase, Kori's favorite play theme was a trip to Star Market. At first the trip consisted of slinging a purse across her shoulder, mounting her rocking horse, and chanting, "Star Market." Two months later a new element was added to the Star Market excursions. Kori recognized that Star Market was a place to buy things. Before mounting the rocking horse, she gathered up a paper bag and her favorite Raggedy Ann. "Go Star Market," she told Raggedy Ann. "Me buy peanut butter, orange juice, cherries."

Within the next few months Kori's language took a quantum leap and her Star Market excursions got much more complicated. "Need a pencil and note pad, going to Star Market. You running out of peanut butter? You need margarine and paper towels?" Kori squiggled some lines on the notebook, gathered up Raggedy Ann, her mother's purse, a paper bag, and a set of keys. Struggling to carry everything in her arms and seating herself on the top of a cardboard carton, Kori scooted herself along the floor. (The carton had replaced the rocking horse as the preferred mode of transportation to Star Market.) "Vroom, vroom, vroom—going to Star Market—mommy running out of peanut butter—mommy running out of paper towels."

As we compare Kori's three renditions of a Star Market excursion, we see changes taking place both in the length of the play episode and in the way Kori uses imitation. In the first episode the imitative component is salient. Kori slings the pocketbook over her shoulder exactly like her mother. As Kori's excursions become more elaborate, there is a change in the way imitation is used. Kori is no longer interested in simply mimicking her mother's actions. Now she is acting out her own routine to express her notion of what going to Star Market means. Star Market is where you buy important things that are good to eat or good for wiping up spills. In other words, as two year olds become more sophisticated, their imaginative play is an interpretation of experience. The imitative elements from earlier play are put into a larger context.

The more elaborate children's pretend play becomes, the more props they need to stage it. One way to collect more props is to spend more time gathering them up. That's what Kori did. Another solution is to get more mileage out of available props. Some of the older two year olds that we visited were particularly good at converting bits and pieces into appropriate props.

"Picnic, going on a picnic," Jennifer announced to her family as she packed up a child-sized picnic basket with books, crayons and a tea set. "Jennifer has never really been on a picnic," her mother explained, "and she seems to get it mixed up with a birthday party." At that moment Jennifer

took out the tea set and set a place for herself and her imaginary guests. Next, she took the crayons out of their box, and stood each crayon up in the criss crosses on the lid. When the last crayon was placed upright on the lid, Jennifer gave an enormous blow. She then instructed her mother to sing Happy Birthday. After the song, Jennifer put the crayons back in the box. "Here's a birthday present," she said to her imaginary friend, "you wanta color?" Jennifer had no problem at all turning the crayons into a candle and back to crayons again. As make believe play becomes elaborated, children make up their own rules and develop their own special symbols.

Another development in imaginative play that we see at two years old is an expanding repertoire of play themes. While the young two year olds play mostly at eating, sleeping, driving and cleaning up, the older two year olds' repertoire of play themes may be considerably larger. They go to the supermarket, the laundromat, the bank, the circus or the zoo. They fish, camp out, go to church or to McDonald's. They are gas station men, garbage men, boatsmen, taxi drivers, mailmen, doctors, or sales clerks.

The increase in the number of play themes is certainly related to the child's expanding life experiences. As children go more places, see more people, and do more things, they have more material to draw on. But perhaps even more important, the addition of new play themes reflects a greater ability to organize and interpret new experiences. A young child is apt to be confused by a trip to the supermarket, and sees it as a sequence of unconnected experiences; a hurried exit from the house, a drive in a car, a place with lots of noise and people, a big basket with cans and boxes and stuff thrown in, a lady who rings a machine. As children return time and time again to the store, they begin to make sense out of these random impressions. Finally, they realize that running out of food, driving to the store, putting food in the basket, giving the cashier money, and bringing the food home are all part of the same event. Each time children play out a new pretend sequence they demonstrate this emerging ability to recreate a sequence and to make sense out of a complex event.

The final and perhaps most critical change in imaginative play within the third year is an increase in the role of language. As children gain more understanding of language, they respond to the suggestions of adults. At the same time their greater ability to use language enables them to direct the action, furnish the dialogue and supply the running commentary in a pretend production. The better the child is at using language, the more elaborate a production can become.

Andrew: Here comes the big truck. Watch out everyone, big truck is coming.
Father: Sorry big truck you have to slow down. You are coming to the toll gate. Here's your ticket, Mr. Truck Driver.
Andrew: Thank you, Mr. Man. Zoom, zoom, going up the mountain. Oops flat tire.
Father: Humm that flat tire looks pretty serious. We better find the jack and jack up your truck.
Andrew: Here's the jack. Fix the tire.
Father: Let's hurry. Looks as if you've got ice cream in your truck. We don't want it to melt.
Andrew: Yeh—got lots of ice cream and chocolate ice cream, and strawberry and more ice cream.
Father: You're making me hungry. How about giving me an ice cream sandwich while we repair this flat tire?

INDIVIDUAL DIFFERENCES

In each home we visited we encouraged the family to describe or demonstrate their favorite pretend themes. As we watched these demonstrations, we became interested in the fact that families not only had favorite themes but also had developed a preferred style of pretending. In some of the families the major way of pretending was role play — adopting the role of someone else or playing out an imaginary experience. In other families the major way of pretending was creating an imaginary world by animating toys or by producing a prop and a story line. For convenience sake we have labeled the first kind of play the actor's style and the second, the producer-director style.

The Actor Style

The actor style play is by far the more popular with the two year old. As an actor the two year old may choose to be himself doing some interesting thing, or else he may select the role of someone else. The someone else that children choose to be most of the time is a mother or father.

As playing a role often requires a costume, it is natural that children pretend to be mother or daddy by dressing themselves up in their parent's clothes. Actually, this interest in dressing up begins very early. As young as eighteen months old youngsters love to sneak into their parents' closet or open up all their drawers. They try on hats, shoes, belts, and scarves. They adorn themselves with beads and bracelets or cover themselves with makeup. In the beginning this dressing up or putting on makeup is highly imitative, but it is the first step to pretending. As the children try out the various items from their parents' wardrobes, they are deciding on the appropriate costume for playing the parent role. The decisions that they make reflect their idea about the critical attributes of a mother or father. The most popular way to play daddy is to wear a belt and shoes and the most popular way to be mommy is to put on beads and carry a purse.

Another very early way of assuming the parent role is to take care of a baby. The baby can be a stuffed animal, a doll, a puppet, a TV character or even a clothespin with a face on it. (Although we have seen older children use cats and dogs as their babies, this is less apt to be true for two year olds.)

Like dress up play, taking care of a baby starts off as highly imitative but evolves over time into a pretend activity. Almost every family we visited reported at least some care-giving play with a doll, puppet or stuffed animal. Let's look at three representative scenes.

Heather at two and a half had a special corner in her bedroom which served as a dining room table for her baby doll, her Disney World characters, and herself. She had the table set for breakfast when we arrived. (For some reason, which Heather's mother had not quite figured out, baby dolls were always undressed before they were brought to the table.)

"Donald, want juice? I give you juice. Want more juice? Want scrambled egg?" (Heather poured some "juice" from the pitcher into the cup, and held it up to Donald's mouth.)

"Mickey Mouse you want juice too, you want egg." (Heather jabbed the scrambled egg with a fork and brought it up to Mickey's mouth.)

Then she turned her attention to the baby dolls.

"Here's bottle, baby doll. Bottle baby doll. All gone — bottle all gone baby doll." (Heather took the bottle away from baby doll, placed her on her shoulder, and burped her tenderly.)

Laura, who is several months younger than Heather, started off her caregiving episode by placing herself and Cookie Monster at a small table in the kitchen. First she fed herself cheerios with an occasional offering to Cookie Monster. Then she picked up the toy telephone and began to jabber. After several seconds, Laura put the telephone to Cookie Monster's ear and warned him in a strict voice "talk couple few minutes."

Angelina, who is about the same age as Laura, chose Howard Johnson's restaurant to begin her pretend play. While they were waiting for dessert to arrive. Angelina's parents got into a conversation and were not paying attention to her. When they looked up, they discovered that Angelina had placed her Crying Tears doll face down on the table and had removed her clothes. "Clean up, clean up, doo," she announced as she wiped Crying Tears' bottom with a paper napkin. After several minutes of vigorous wiping, Angelina unfolded the napkin and covered Crying Tears, "Ah, ah go sleep," but apparently Crying Tears was not quite ready for sleep. Angelina picked her up suddenly, crunched the napkin and went back to wiping her bottom. "Clean up doo, clean doo, all up," she continued in a still louder voice.

As we examine these three rather typical examples of doll play, we can see the two year old's idea of what the caregiver's role consists of. In the homes we visited the children were more apt to associate the caregiver role with the mother. For most two year olds the critical part of being a mother is to cook, to talk on the telephone, and to take care of the baby. In the various homes we visited, dolls were fed, diapered, dressed, read to, taken for walks, put on the toilet and given a bath. They had their face washed, their rear end wiped, their temperature taken, their hair washed and brushed. They were taught how to read and write, how to slide down a slide, and how to do a sommersault. They were kissed, hugged, scolded, spanked and placed face down in the corner. Watching the two year olds carrying out these play routines gives us a glimpse of the child's impression of what a parent does. Interestingly enough we found that our "children-parents" are harsher disciplinarians than their own parents. Parents who almost never used spanking as a disciplinarian technique were surprised to see their children energetically spanking their dolls.

The children that we have described so far played the role of caregiver by animating a doll. Another common way to try out this role is to switch roles with a parent and make the parent be the baby.

"You the baby," Jimmy announced to his father who had just come from work. "Sit down right here. I bring you a drink of juice. You like the juice?" Jimmy asked as he fed his father a cup full of air.

"No," his father muttered. "This juice is terrible; it's sour. I want a bunch of grapes."

"Here some grapes," Jimmy continued sweetly, after a quick trip to the hall which apparently served as a kitchen.

"Oh bother," his father complained, "these grapes have seeds in them. I think I would like to have some green seedless grapes."

Unperturbed, Jimmy sent back to his storehouse in the hall, "here some gweenless gwapes, daddy."

All of the children who took the parent's role did not put up this well with their demanding babies.

Erik decided one evening that he was the mother and the rest of the family, Mother, Daddy, Grandma and Grandpa were all babies.

Erik distributed "blankets" to each member of his cast, "Bedtime everybody go to sleep."

"This is no blanket. This is a diaper. I want a blanket," complained Grandpa.

"Okay you take this blanket," Erik said pulling away the blanket from his father and giving it to Grandpa.

"I want my blanket back," Erik's daddy howled in mock rage.

Then his mother joined in, "I want a bigger blanket. This one is too small."

Standing in the middle of the floor with his hands on his hips Erik said firmly, "Try to be quiet and take your naps."

Just as the children in many of our families associated mothers with caregivers, they associated fathers with going off to work. The most frequent way of pretending to be the father was to drive a car.

Susan: "Need my lunch box. No butter please—gotta watch my clesterall."

Mother: "Your what?—oh, your cholesterol—ok I didn't put any butter on your sandwich." (Hands Susan the empty lunch box.)

Susan: "Bye, going to work — got to hurry." (Gets on "Big Wheel and drives from the kitchen to the living room.) "Vroom, vroom, vroom — got to go to work."

The play never really went further than this. It may be that Susan, like many other children, wasn't quite sure what daddy did when he went to work.

Another attribute that some of our children attached to the father role was being the fixer. When we first came into the house, Frank was on the porch inserting the barrel of a toy pistol into a screw head on the window screen. As we watched him, he moved systematically from screen to screen inserting the gun into each screw head and giving it a quick twist. The entire operation was completed without a word. After each of the screws was tightened. Frank went to work on the caulking. Using his gun now as a caulking tool he went about sealing the cracks in the screens. We asked Frank's mother how this intense interest in fixing got started. The only thing that she could figure out was that her own father would come to the house about once a month, tool kit in hand, and fix everything that needed fixing. Frank would trail his grandfather for the entire day cooperating as well as he could in each of the repair jobs. Apparently Frank had decided that a man's role is to fix things.

The only other attempt we observed of playing out the father role was a departure scene.

Mandy picked up her father's briefcase and a pencil and walked toward the door.

Mandy: "Got to go to work. Got a busy day. Got to say goodbye and go to work."

Mother: "Goodbye, Daddy. Have a good day at work. See you later.'"

Mandy: "Goodbye. Got to go to work with all of my papers. Got to work with my briefcase. Goodbye."

Mandy's final goodbye seemed to signify the end of her knowledge of what daddies do as much as it signalled a salutation.

It appears that when children take the caregiver role they have a fairly clear, although stereotyped, idea of what should be done. The provider role, on the other hand, was not elaborated. As parents share the roles of caregiver and provider, we would expect that children's ideas of what mother and fathers do will change accordingly. But with young children, the caregiver role that is carried out within the home will continue to be understood better than the more remote role of provider.

A second point that needs to be made about two year olds is that girls and boys try out both the mother and father role regardless of their own sex. This suggests that it is a good time for parents to provide props that will facilitate playing either role. Boys enjoy dolls, cooking utensils and tea sets and girls enjoy cars, trucks, and tool kits. At three and four we may see some rejection of opposite sex-typed toys as children insist on taking the role of their same sexed parent.

Next to being a mother or daddy, the most popular role was pretending to be a doctor. Doctor play is particularly interesting to watch because it provides some insights into a two year old's perception of what a doctor does. Two year olds who played doctor without having any props always began the game by making the patient (a parent or stuffed animal) lie down on his back. The patient was thumped on various parts of his anatomy, then told to get up and given medicine. When a child had a doctor's kit at his disposal, the examination became more extensive.

Stephanie, who is just four years old, picked up her two year old sister and stretched her out on the sofa. "You're the baby and I'm the doctor. I'm gonna make you all better so don't you move." Amy obediently waited while Stephanie poked her with each of the instruments and gave her some just-pretend shots. At Stephanie's suggestion she even made pretend crying noises at the appropriate moments. As soon as "Doctor" Stephanie turned her attention away, Amy took over the doctor role. Her mother was elected as patient and Amy used each instrument in succession just as her sister had done. At the end of the examination Amy gave her mother medicine and an imaginary balloon. The whole examination had proceeded with little conversation except that Amy provided the appropriate cue when it was time for her patient to cry.

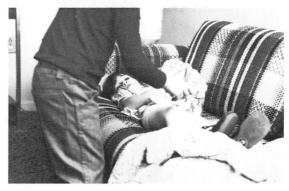

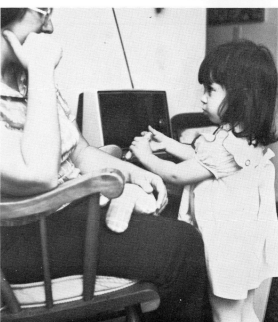

Another role which many of our actor type children played was being a waiter or waitress. Because this role is quite dependent on language, it was not very popular with less verbal children. As a matter of fact the restaurant role works best when an adult participates.

Andy and his father provide a good demonstration. "I'd like a large green hot dog with corn ears," requested daddy. "No man," Andy replied. "We don't got no hot dogs in this restaurant. You want a hamburger?" Father, "No hot dogs! What kind of a restaurant is this? Do you have a cucumber and ice cream sandwich?" The game continued with much laughter.

As we watched children assume different roles, we recognized that the amount of elaboration of a particular role reflected the child's degree of familiarity with the role. Theresa had an older sister who was in kindergarten. When Sue left for school, Theresa sat Curious George at the table. "I'm the teacher," she told Curious George. "Time for lunch, open up your lunch box up, eat your lunch right this minute."

Tania, who goes to a small church group three times a week, had a clearer idea about what teachers do. Like Patti, she arranged her dolls at the table. "No, no Baby Boo, no pushin. How many times I got to tell you? No pushin. Sit in the corner and don't you move."

Terry and Tommy, who had a fair amount of exposure to older children, often pretended to be policemen. In what appeared to be an imitation of older children's play, they pointed their toy guns at each other and went bang, bang. They then began a back and forth verbal barrage. "You go to jail." "No, you go to jail." "No, you go to jail."

As we thought about the varous roles that children tried out, we recognized that many of the roles they selected were actually extensions of the caretaker role. Being a teacher, storekeeper, doctor, or waitress is in a sense placing the attributes of the caretaker mother role in a larger context. And being a garbage man, a doctor, or an airplane pilot involves extending the fixer-driver father role attributes in a similar way. It seems that the child is using a role play situation to interpret a new experience. By placing this new experience in a familiar context, that is, by finding the parallels between the new and the old, the child comes to understand these more remote experiences.

While some of our actor type children increase their repertoire of imaginative play themes by taking different roles, others take a different approach. Instead of changing roles, they add variety to their play themes by pretending that something interesting is about to happen — a birthday party, a ride on a boat, a trip to Minnesota, to the beach, or to the laundromat. With very few exceptions, children who go on pretend trips never reach their destination. As a matter of fact, most of the time they don't even get on the road. The high point of an excursion is the preparation.

"Going to the beach," Jennifer announced as she sorted through the box of stuff in the corner of the room.

"Need the keys. I'm not taking the bus to the beach, going by car. You want to go to the beach?" she asked her doll wrapping it in a diaper and stuffing it into the carriage.

"I want to go to the beach," Dolly answered in Jennifer's high squeaky voice.

"Wait for me," said Jennifer to doll. "I've got to get packed up." Jennifer got busy filling a paper bag with an assortment of beach supplies — a toothbrush, a Green Stamp catalogue, an empty milk carton, a string of beads, a piggy bank and a Sesame Street record.

"Got to dress me," she insisted as she struggled to get her arm in the sleeve of a smock. Satisfied with her own outfit, Jennifer found a hat for her doll and a hat for her younger brother. "Want to be the daddy?" she asked her brother in a solicitous voice.

A few minutes later Jennifer turned her attention to the food supply for the picnic. "I'm making hamburgers," Jennifer explained.

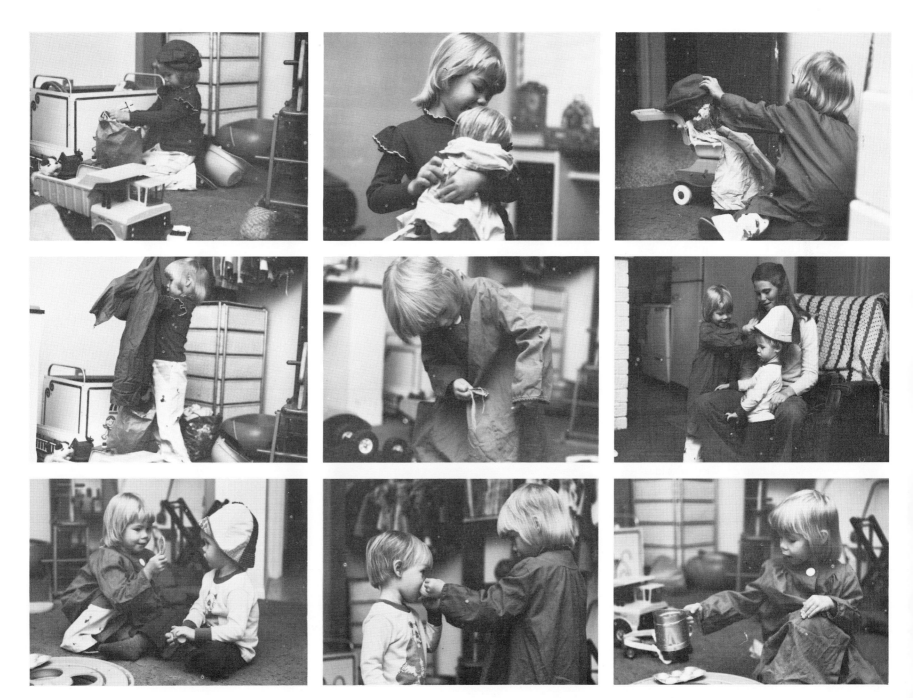

Kori's version of the trip combined several trip stories into one:

Kori: (Sitting on a push toy truck and pushing herself back and forth in front of the mirror.) "Where pink keys? Turning on Honda. Taking mommy to work."

Mother: "Okay, I'm ready. Let's go."

Kori: "We at work now. Get out mommy. Do your work. I have to go home do my work." (Pushes the truck back and forth in front of the mirror several times.) "Time to get you mommy. We got to go get daddy."

Mother: "Where's daddy?"

Kori: "Daddy at work. Daddy in Arlington. Got to pick up daddy. Get in daddy. Got to pick up Nana. (Again moves back and forth several times in front of the mirror.) Nana, you can sit in my lap. Got to get something." (Runs to the other room and gets Raggedy Ann and Fringe and then gets back on truck.)

Mother: "Are we ready to go now?"

Kori: "We ready to go. We at Florida."

Even though Jennifer didn't make it to the beach, and Kori never did anything once she got to Florida, both children devoted a good bit of time to a single play theme. Many of the two year olds we watched were much more episodic in their play. They skipped from role to role and theme to theme with no attention to continuity. Angela provides a delightful example of this kind of versatile play.

When we first came into the house, Angela was riding her Fisher Price Giraffe on the back porch. "Hurry up horsey, hurry up horsey," she chanted. As soon as she saw us, she picked up her horse and carried him into the living room. "Thirsty horsey," she asked as she offered him a drink out of a paper cup. Then she turned the horse on its side, felt it to see if it was dry, took its temperature with a spoon, and diapered it with a kitchen towel. When her mother turned on the music, she picked up the horse and danced with it around the room. At the end of the record she turned her attention to the horse's wheels. For some reason they reminded her of a barbecue grill. Angela flipped an imaginary hamburger on the grill. "Hungry mommy, want lunch? You want ketchup?"

Producer-Director Style

So far we have been looking at a style of imaginative play in which the child is the actor portraying the role of a familiar character, or playing out some interesting event. In either situation the child pretends by placing himself directly in the imaginary scene.

Another style of imaginative play that we see during this age is the producer-director style. In contrast to the actor, the producer-director's activity is somewhat more detached. The child stands back from the action and directs his pretend world. Sometimes the child concentrates on arranging an imaginary set, at other times he animates a cast of miniature characters. The favorite props for this activity are standard commercial toys — cars, and trucks, farm animals, Fisher Price People, doll house furniture or Sesame Street characters.

Kori had just returned from a trip to Drumland Farm. Her mother had prearranged a farm scene on her bedroom floor using a Fisher Price farm set. Kori examined the scene with intense interest. For several minutes she clutched her hands in a gesture of quiet excitement. "The horse is thirsty," Kori's mother suggested. Kori crouched down on the carpet. She put the farmer inside the toy wagon, and pulled the wagon around in a circle. "Here water, horse," she said for the farmer who was pulling the wagon. "Hm, thank you — glup, glup, glup," answered the horse. "Want more water, want some dinner? Pig want water too?" Kori systematically pulled the wagon around the farm yard, providing the dialogue for both the farmer and the animals.

Matthew, like Kori, frequently assumed the producer-director role in an imaginative play routine. Matthew had been playing on the floor with Kermit the frog, a teddy bear and a basket ball hoop. When Kermit got stuck in the basketball hoop, his mother initiated the imaginative play theme by talking to the frog. "Oh Kermit, you are hurt. Do you need to go to the doctor?" Matthew immediately began talking for Kermit, making his voice high and squeaky. "Yes, I'm hurt. Take me to the doctor." The doctor conveniently enough turned out to be Teddy Bear. Matthew lowered his voice in order to sound like Teddy Bear. "You got hurt? Need a band-aid, need medicine? Here, eat this purple medicine. Now Kermit's leg is alright. He's going to practice jumping. Here he comes over the bed. He's going to jump through the tire—watch this. Now he's going to jump way up to the ceiling."

As we examine Kori's orchestration of the Drumland Farm scene and Matthew's maneuvers with Kermit the Frog, it is obvious that both Kori and Matthew are relying on an adult to help with some of the dialogue. It takes a fair amount of sophistication to be a director-producer when all of the characters have a speaking part. It's not surprising that our director-producers are often perfectly satisfied with issuing stage directions to the actors.

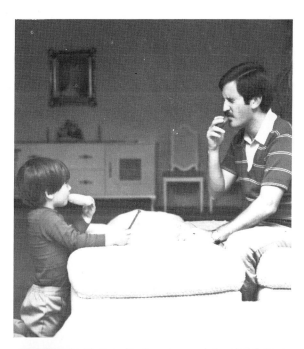

Lynn was playing with a Fisher Price Merry-Go-Round and a set of miniature people. For some unknown reason she had named her little people Mopsy, Dopsy, and Gopsy. "Your turn Gopsy," she said picking up the little girl. "Your turn on merry-go-round. No pushing. Gotta take turns. Gotta share. Dopsy's turn. Gotta give Dopsy turn. Here Mopsy you fit, too. No, no Mopsy, no pushing."

A very early rendition of the director role may not even be as sophisticated as Lynn's merry-go-round play. Several of the children we watched set up the stage with miniature characters without adding any dialogue. Madeline, who is a relatively non-verbal two year old, had a package of miniature salt and pepper shakers and a set of tootsie cars. While we were watching, Madeline lined up her cars and put one or two of the shakers beside each other. We really weren't sure whether or not she was pretending until her older brother asked if he could have a car. Madeline put her arms protectively around the fleet and answered in a cross voice, "no, no fill up." "Oh, her brother interpreted, "she's filling her cars with gas."

The producer-director style does not necessarily require miniature people, animals, or elaborate props. It can begin with basic raw materials — blocks, crayon and paper, a ball of clay, or perhaps just words. Once children grasp the idea that they can set the rules in imaginative play and things can become whatever they want them to be, they are ready to devise their own props, create their own scenes and write their own storylines. The most common example of pretending with basic materials is block play. Although occasionally children play with blocks as a manipulative activity, building towers and knocking them down, most two year old block play includes some kind of pretending.

Chris was sitting on the floor surrounded by a set of alphabet blocks.

Chris: Here a cookie, here another cookie, here lots of cookies."
Chris' mother: "Yes, you have lots of cookies. Should we pack our lunch and go on a picnic."
Chris: "Here another cookie. Here a hambugger. Hambugger hot."

Like Chris, many of the children we visited used the blocks for pretend play. Blocks of different shapes were used as candy, dog biscuits, money, cameras and microphones. Blocks were placed end on end to make trains, parades and traffic jams. Like the actor child who gets so busy putting on the costume that nothing else happens, the director-producer can get so absorbed with setting out the props that the play ends there.

A few of the children that we visited used pencils, crayons, or chalk to set the scene for pretending. Although they were not very adept at managing their implement, they were great with interpretation.

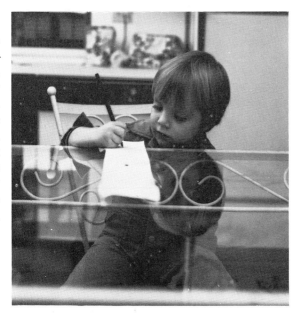

Kori sat at the kitchen table with a pencil and a sheet of paper. In contrast to her usual style of making little squiggles, she made two circles—one on top of the other. She continued to work intently on the drawing placing several circles inside the upper circles and a spiral in the center of the lower circle. "That's a picture of me," Kori explained to her mother. "See me eyes, and me nose, and there is me mouth." Her mother asked about the spiral inside the lower circle. Kori responded, "that's me tummy hurts just a little bit."

It's important to recognize that Kori did not start off with the idea of drawing herself with a tummy ache. Few two year olds can do more than draw circles, lines and squiggles. What happens is that they begin to make squiggles on the paper and then get interested in talking about the squiggles. It's a kind of ex post facto interpretation. This became apparent when Kori finished the tummy ache drawing and went back to making squiggles. "Look mommy, found a no good banana." Her mother looked. Sure enough, there was a banana shaped squiggle with a black spot on it. "Throw it in the garbage," Kori insisted as she pretended to pick the banana off the sheet.

As children develop a facility with language, pretend scenes can be created using only words. This is particularly true with children who have been read to a lot or who have heard a lot of stories. Kori was putting "This Girl" to sleep:

"Want a story, This Girl. I will tell you a story. One morning This Girl woke and wanted to go to the zoo. She got some milk and a sandwich because she was just a little hungry, and I got my Honda and Honda went vrooming all the way to the zoo. We at the zoo. We got out from Honda and went into the zoo. Then I had to do my work. I have a lot of work."

In contrast to Kori's story, which is a recap of everyday experiences, Matthew's stories were much more fantastic. "A big monster lives in daddy's office and he's large and brown." Matthew waited for an invitation to continue and was satisfied when we asked if he had seen the monster lately. "I slammed the door so that the monster couldn't bite me," Matthew went on. "Maybe it's a friendly monster and you could give it a toy," we suggested. Matthew went off to try and came back with a long explanation. "I got a toy airplane. Big monster pulling on airplane—pulling, pulling on toy airplane. I poked it with a pencil. Just like that I poked it with a pencil."

A favorite time for children to tell stories is on the way to sleep or when they are alone in a room. This means that parents often miss their child's most creative stories. Gregory had been misbehaving and was sent into his mother's room as a punishment. He went into the room quietly. After a few minutes his mother decided he had been punished long enough and went into the room to retrieve him. As she entered the room, she found Gregory holding up a picture of his grandparents and babbling on about going on a trip and climbing an apple tree. She tried to get him to continue but he dismissed her immediately. "Go away mommy, I'm talking to Nana and Papa."

Whether or not we can figure out the stories children invent, we can be fairly certain about two things. First, once children adopt a story line their stories become repetitive. All of Kori's stories begin with getting out of bed, having something to eat, and going for a ride in Honda. Gregory's stories always include some sort of calamity with the blue monster. Second, we can be certain that none of the stories children tell are completely spontaneous inventions. The stories combine bits and pieces of stories that were told or read to them with some elements pulled out of their own experience.

When children tell stories, they sometimes lose the distinction between real and just pretend. What begins as a story may gain so much creditability during the telling that a child ends up believing his own inventions. In the beginning Matthew knew his story about the monster in daddy's office was a pretense, but as each new detail was added, he became increasingly serious. Parents may feel that a two year old is lying in this kind of situation. However, most children at two years old are not capable of telling a deliberate lie. They are just temporarily confused about the difference between real and just made up.

There are times when it's difficult to draw a line between actor type play and director type play. This is especially true when there are dolls or puppets on the scene. Is the child who is telling Big Bird to eat up his spinach giving out a stage direction or playing the part of caregiver? Furthermore, at two years old there is a kind of fluidity in an imaginative play sequence. At one moment the child is telling the engineer to drive the train under the tunnel and pick up the passengers. At the next moment he is the engineer, making "toot-toot" noises, and turning an imaginary steering wheel.

Our general impression is that the child who prefers the actor style is physically active, exploratory, energetic and impulsive. The producer-director type is apt to be somewhat more reflective—planning out strategies and developing new ideas. It would be interesting to follow some of these children over time. Will the children who prefer the actor style grow up to be outgoing and social, while the producer-director type grow up to be more reflective and introvertive?

REASONS FOR PRETENDING

In attempting to describe the various kinds of imaginative play we find in two to three year olds, we have selected examples that are particularly striking. These examples are not typical of all the families we visited. As a matter of fact, we found many children who were not interested in imaginative play at all. We wondered about these children. Will they play imaginatively when they are a little older? Are there some children who never really do get interested in imaginative play? Recognizing the range of individual differences both in the style and the amount of imaginative play, we are faced with some difficult questions: Why do children pretend? What purpose does it serve? Is imaginative play a critical factor in emotional and cognitive development?

Making Sense Out of The World

Imaginative play is often described as the child's way of making sense out of his world. As children play and replay familiar events, they understand them better. If we look at the themes of early imaginative play, this explanation seems to be plausible.

Of all the imaginative play themes the food theme is by far the most popular. At just over a year we see the beginning of pretend eating. One toddler lifts an empty cup to her lips and gives her daddy a pretend bit of her dinner; a second toddler makes believe that she is picking a grape off the fruit design of her mother's blouse. By the middle of the second year the eating theme undergoes its first expansion and children become interested in the preparation of food. They make cookies out of sand, mix a birthday cake in an empty bowl, or crack pretend eggs on the side of a cake pan. A further extension, usually in the early two's, involves serving the food. This is the well known tea party stage in which the child plays hostess to people, dolls or stuffed animals.

From this point on the food theme can be expanded in several directions. Many children at two and a half or three get interested in pretending to buy food at the grocery store. Some children recognize that before you go to buy food you have to make a list of what you're running out of. Other children get interested in where the money to buy food comes from, and may stop off at the bank on the way to the grocery. Still other children take a different tactic. They go on a picnic, plan a barbecue or eat out in a restaurant.

Looking at the various expansions and extensions of the food theme, we recognize how children use pretending to make sense out of their daily experiences. Food is elaborated more than other themes because children have so much experience with the process of buying, preparing and eating food. In contrast, themes like fireman, policeman, or paramedic are not expanded very much at this age because the experiences of children with these roles are very limited. During the next few years, as they extend their experiences and begin to absorb more information from books and television, the children will elaborate more remote themes.

As children become more sophisticated in their imaginative play, they learn to make jokes out of their pretending. These jokes usually emerge from pretend themes that have been repeated so often they have become a kind of game. In the beginning this pretend eating tends to be quite serious, but eventually the pretense is so well established that it becomes a matter of play. Clarence, for example, looked at his father and laughed as he took pretend bites out of his father's tie and a magazine cover.

Eating jokes can even evolve into pretend rituals that are repeated on a daily basis. "What kind of ice cream you want," Erik asked. "Broccoli," answered his father, who knew this was Erik's favorite vegetable. Erik pretended to scoop up imaginary ice cream and poke it into an imaginary cone in his other hand, "Here you are," he said, handing the ice cream cone to his father. "Mm, yum, what kind do you want," his father asked as he switched the roles. "Spaghetti," Erik ordered. His father went through the motions of making the ice cream cone. "Oh yes, we have some good spaghetti ice cream today."

When children make pretend jokes, it is a clear sign that they are learning to recognize the difference between reality and fantasy. Another sign is the use of the word "pretend" or some similar word. When children use the word "pretend" in an appropriate way, they are making a distinction between reality and fantasy. Parents who introduce a word like "pretend" as they play with their two year olds usually find that the children pick up the term rather quickly. Once children are familiar with "pretend," parents can help them make further distinctions between reality and fantasy in confusing situations. Imaginative thought has both power and limitations. It can create a powerful imaginary experience, but not directly change the real world. By fostering imaginative play we can help children appreciate this paradox.

Compensating For Feelings of Inadequacy

Another explanation that is given for imaginative play is that children are compensating for some feeling of inadequacy. They may be trying to overcome feelings of anxiety and powerlessness, or they may be seeking a companion to provide support and counteract the loneliness that comes with growing up. Sometimes they just want to replay an exciting experience that cannot be repeated in real life.

An important way of getting rid of feelings of inadequacy is to gain control of fear. The kinds of fear that plague the two year old often appear to parents to be irrational. Parents told us of two year olds who were afraid of butterflies, beards, egg shells, fire sirens, band aids and Santa Claus. Zachary would not go to sleep at night because he was afraid that a cow would jump on the roof and crash into his bedroom.

As we think about the two year old's growth, we recognize that these fears are the products of the child's ability to create pictures in his mind and to imagine about things that are not present. The same developmental advancement that gives the child the power to play out imaginative themes also makes him fearful. He thinks up scary pictures, and animates all sorts of inanimate things—stuffed animals, trees, the moon, or clothes hanging up in the dark.

Gregory was terribly afraid of lions. Several times during the night he would run into his parents' bedroom, screaming that a lion was after him. At the same time he was insistent that his mother and daddy read a story about Johnny Lion before he went to sleep. He even took a little stuffed tiger to bed with him at night. At first his parents thought it might be better to take away both the book and the tiger, but then they realized that this pretend experience was a healthy way for Gregory to cope with his fear.

In some of the homes we visited parents were aware of how imaginative play could overcome fears and they used it for just this purpose. Ginny got soap in her eyes during a shampooing and became terrified of having her hair washed. Even the sight of a shampoo bottle was enough to set off a tantrum. One day her dad got an idea. He brought Ginny a doll with hair and accidentally, on purpose, spilled chocolate syrup on it. Ginny was delighted with the idea of washing the syrup out of the doll's hair. After using a large bottle of shampoo on her doll, Ginny became less fearful of the shampooing process.

Not all the fears that children have to cope with are imaginative. There are many real life experiences that are scary or unpleasant from a child's point of view. Over and over during our visits parents reported an increase in doctor play before and after a doctor's appointment. Stuffed animals and dolls were stripped, thumped, poked, and fed medicine. Even children who appeared to do nothing but scream in the doctor's office were apparently aware of the entire sequence and could reenact it with their dolls.

With their new powers of imagination, two year old children often exaggerate dangers that parents have pointed out. For example, parents who emphasize that bees are dangerous to handle may find their two year old generalizing this fear to all flying insects. If a little bee is a matter of concern, imagine the danger of a much larger butterfly. In addition the fears of toddlers sometimes are carried over into this age period and intensified by imagination. A child who was afraid of dogs jumping on him may begin to whimper at the mere sight of a dog across the street. The faintest sound of a distant siren may cause alarm in a child who previously was afraid of loud noises. In cases like these, the imagination of children runs away with them. The vividness of an imaginary danger blocks out their ability to recognize the real situation.

Parents usually feel good about a two year old's ability to pretend. On the other hand, they are concerned when children acquire "irrational" fears. Yet there is a strong overlap between the two. Jon's pretending was elaborate at an early age. At the same time he was afraid of thunder, cement trucks, the beach, and cats. He had been terrified during a recent trip to Disney World. Like Jon, two year old children who are very imaginative tend to be fearful. The one goes with the other.

Another way children use imagination to compensate for the deficiencies of the real world is to create an imaginary companion. Almost every child we visited had a favorite doll, stuffed animal, or security blanket. These loved items kept the child company in new and strange situations. At an early age children are not very selective about the kind of thing they choose for a companion. Several of our young two year olds were attached to such odd items as screwdrivers, shampoo bottles, blankets, egg beaters, old diapers, and whisk brooms. These objects seemed to be almost animate. The children would insist on taking them along on rides, bringing them to the table, and going to sleep with them.

Occasionally parents even hear children talking to these strange companions. "Bye-bye, have to go to store now," Jason said to a new pair of shoes in his closet.

The animation of unlikely objects seems to disappear between two and three, but the animation of dolls and stuffed animals gets even stronger. At Halloween Erik adopted a large skeleton decoration as his companion. "Look at shoe," he exclaimed with excitement, pointing to the bones in the skeleton's foot. "Mr. Skeleton nice man, he want eat too," Erik said. After a large chair had been provided and Mr. Skeleton draped over it, Erik decided that this new companion wanted to eat soap. Later in the day it looked like the skeleton had been forgotten on the floor, but Erik informed his parents, "try to be quiet, Skeleton taking nap."

A common practice of two year olds who use their dolls as friends, is to make the doll imitate their own activity. If they go down the slide, the doll goes down the slide. If they have a bit of pretend ice cream, the doll must hold her own spoon and feed herself ice cream.

Just as children use their pretending to meet their social needs, they use imaginative play to compensate for their lack of control over events in the real world. Most of the time things happen to young children. They are told when to get up and when to sleep; when, where, how, and what to eat; when and where to go to the bathroom, etc. In a pretend game the children can spank, scold, and punish their dolls, or bring them to a party without clothes on. They set the rules, boss the characters, and control the consequences.

Robbie liked to dump his miniature toy people into the bathtub. Then he proceeded to order them around—"time to go swimming—time to get out—time to take a nap—time to eat lunch." Insubordination led to harsh consequences. One little boy did not get out of the bathtub when he was told and subsequently drowned. Other characters were spanked for not eating their hamburgers, and Ernie and Bert were left behind because they didn't pay attention to the command, "time to get in the car."

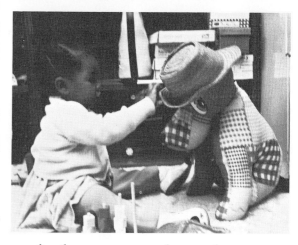

Another way to control events is to recreate special experiences through pretend play. A two year old can go on a picnic with Sesame Street friends and eat nothing but candy and cookies. He can organize an endless succession of birthday parties or camping trips, or talk on the phone as long as he wants.

WAYS TO FOSTER IMAGINATIVE PLAY

Among the families we visited we found very definite attitudes about imagination. In a small minority of the families imaginative play was frowned upon. It was thought of as a mechanism for avoiding the truth, and children who indulged in imaginative play were scolded for telling lies. A second group of parents, also a small minority, tolerated imaginative play but felt that it took away time from more important things like learning numbers and letters. A third group, and by far the majority, felt that imaginative play was important and sought out ways to encourage it. We were especially interested in these families and tried to identify characteristics that these families had in common.

1. There were adults or older children who had a special interest and talent for playing imaginatively with the two year olds.
2. There were toys and materials available that could be played with in a variety of ways.
3. There was a place to play where the child could gather props and carry out a play sequence.

The Role of the Adult

For a two year old the greatest inducement for pretending is to play with an adult or older child who enjoys it. As we visited with different families, it was easy to identify the parents who were especially interested in their child's imaginative play. These parents described with obvious pleasure the pretend games that they and their children enjoyed together.

Brian's family is a clear example of a family that took advantage of their youngster's readiness to play imaginatively. As you walk into the family room, the first thing that strikes your eye is a giant wooden structure that takes up a good third of the room. This structure is a playhouse built to order by Brian's father. It can serve as a store, a castle, a jail, a puppet theater, or just a good hiding place. Obviously, the family has a great time with it.

One of the most interesting facets of watching parents play with their children is identifying the parent's play style. Like children, the parents that we visited seem to have developed a preferred style of imaginative play. Some parents preferred to be actors. They participated in a very direct way in their child's pretend themes. Others were definitely the producer-director types, gathering props, suggesting dialogue, drawing pictures, telling stories, or making up rhymes and songs. And finally, we found the "appreciative audience" parents—the parents who loved to watch their children's pretend activities but did not participate actively.

Parents who were skilled in actor type play knew how to be opportunistic. At just the right moment they asked a question or made a comment that served to initiate an imaginative play sequence.

Steven was sitting on top of his red car making a vrum vrum noise. His father had been talking to us.

"Hello Mr. Steven, I see you are out in your red corvette. Are you running a bit low on gas?"

"Fill er up please," Mr. Steven responded. (Obviously this was not the first time father and son had enacted this scene.)

Steven's father pretended to fill the car with gas. "Do you want me to check the tires? Your right rear looks a bit low on air." Steven watched as his father pretended to check the tires.

Steven, "How much I owe you?"

Steven's father, "$10.00 even." Steven pretended to take the money out of his pocket and put it in his father's hand. He drove off with a rumming sound but was back ten seconds later for a repeat performance.

Laura's mother, like Steven's father, very much enjoyed the actor type play. Her particular forte was pantomine. While we were there she and Laura played a very elaborate pretend game using elaborate gestures and very few words. Laura was playing in her outgrown cradle which her mother had placed on the floor. As Laura climbed into it, she said, "boat." Her mother took advantage of the moment. "Let's go on a boat trip," she suggested climbing in the cradle beside Laura. "We'll see if we can catch a fish. Throw out your rod." At this point Laura's mother went through an elaborate pantomime in which she threw out her line, caught a fish, tossed it into the boat, and wiped off the splashes from her face and arms. Laura was very attentive. Obviously, she could not follow the whole routine, but she enjoyed watching her mother.

In many of the homes we visited an older sister or brother joined in the actor type play. In most cases this worked very well. The two year old was so delighted to be included in the act that he was willing to accept whatever part he was assigned—the baby, the mother or father, the patient, the student, the pet animal, or the performer. We did not come across play sequences where the two year olds were given a speaking part. Even as the performer, they were not expected to do any more than twist and turn when the older sibling played the music and made the announcements. As the baby or the patient, their part was limited to crying on cue. As father they were expected to carry the props to wherever they were going.

In most cases the two year old accepted a passive role while the older child was providing the cues. But at the first opportunity the younger child took over the abandoned props and played his sibling's role. We are amazed at how adept our two year olds were in following a play routine. We watched Harris take over the role of teacher when his sister left the room. "This is a "A," he told the bionic woman as he showed her a "W." Say it now, say "A." Say "A" nice and loud so I hear you."

Many of the parents who enjoyed playing the director part helped set up an elaborate playscape, a Sesame Street Playground, a gasoline station, a zoo, or perhaps a camp out. Others selected a less grandiose stage setting and concentrated their efforts on making puppets or animals talk. Katie's mother is a fairly typical director mother. She begins the play episode by picking up a small plastic horse.

"Hello horse, are you hungry? Would you like to have some hay? Here's the hay over here. Jump over the fence."

Katie takes over at this point. "Jump fence, jump over fence. You want me give you hay? You like it? You want more hay?"

The older siblings we watched were not usually as effective as parents in being director play models. Although they started off playing with the two year old, they were apt to get so involved in playing that they took over the play completely. After all, a play can't have two directors.

Being an effective director model requires not only knowing when to let the child take over the play but also being sensitive to the play level of the child. If the play is too elaborate or too exotic, the child will lose interest. One of the families that we visited had invested in an expensive electric train set with all kinds of clever gadgets and accessories. The two year old enjoyed making the train start and stop, but never went beyond manipulation. After a week or so the train was put up into the attic waiting for the child to grow into it.

Timothy's mother was a most effective director type. She was sensitive to Timothy's inquisitiveness and his interest in replaying a new experience. Timothy had gone on a picnic with his grandfather at a state park. When Timothy came home, he went to the play corner of the family room where all his toys were kept. There on a low table he found his little Sesame Street people. Big Bird, Ernie and Bert were arranged around the picnic table. (The picnic table was a red and white checked paper napkin.) Beside the picnic table there was a small basket full of bits of junk. With no encouragement Timothy began to direct the show.

"Want a hamburger, Ernie," Timothy asked as he served Ernie a delicious cork coaster. "No, Ernie, no more ketchup. You want ice tea? We don't got ice tea. Want hot dog? Mommy, need cook it." Timothy was now pulling his mommy's jeans.

"Need what?" his mother asked, puzzled by the request.

"Need cook it," Timothy repeated insistently. "Need cook it — hot dog."

"Oh, you need to cook your hot dog. You need a barbecue."

"Yes, need cook it."

Timothy was delighted that his mother understood him. He was perfectly satisfied with the empty juice can that she gave him to use as a barbecue.

As we watched Timothy and his mother, it was obvious that this kind of pretending was quite typical. Although Timothy's mother did not get into the act, she knew just the kind of props that would get Timothy started. She also accepted Timothy's rules for pretending. Invisible hot dogs were fine to serve to Bert and Ernie as long as they had been cooked on an appropriate grill.

Many of the parents who enjoyed the producer-director type play found creative ways to initiate imaginative games with their youngster.

They drew pictures, sang songs, and made up bedtime stories. Children are not at all particular about the artistic quality of their parents' drawing, although parents may resist drawing for their children because they themselves are dissatisfied with their products. The parents in our study who were willing to make simple crayon or chalk drawings found it a marvelous way to encourage imaginative play.

Chris had a small desk with a chalk board top. One of his favorite activities was telling his father what to draw and then talking about it.

"Draw a fish, Daddy. Draw a fish in the water. Make a boat. Jump fish in the boat. Me make the fish fall out. Me make the fish gone in the water."

As in drawing, the quality of a song doesn't matter at all to the two year old. Even monotone parents can enjoy an appreciative audience. Two year olds show a new awareness of verbal humor as parents add variations and additions to familiar routines.

"Rock a bye Christopher
in a hot dog bun.
When the wind blows,
then he will have fun."

Producer-director parents also encouraged imaginative play by initiating building activities. They helped their children use blocks to create simple structures—a road for the car to go along, a fence to keep the pigs in, a bed for Mickey Mouse, a bridge for the boat to go under. Each time the children mastered one of these block arrangements, their potential for pretending increased. They could build a balance beam for the playground, pumps for the gasoline station, or a swimming pool for rubber ducky. As the child's skill grew, parents could step back and enjoy their child's creativity.

The Props Whether parents participate as an actor, a producer-director, or just an appreciative audience, their personal involvement in the child's imaginative play is a critical factor. But besides this personal involvement they also can set the state for imaginative play by providing appropriate props. We have developed two lists. The first list includes those props that appeared to be most conducive to actor type play. The second list includes those props that especially encourage producer-director type play.

As children become more and more interested in collecting props to accompany a play theme, parents are given an opportunity to express their own creativity by helping to set the stage. It was interesting to discover how many different ways parents found to fill a picnic basket. One of our parents cut pictures of food out of a magazine. A second parent saved jello, raisin, and small cereal boxes. Another parent used bread dough to make a variety of play foods. But, no matter how much fun parents have helping their child with props, this prop gathering stage presents problems. One parent complained about lost keys, extension cords, credit cards, and pot lids appearing in the oddest places.

The props that work best for actor type play correspond with the ways the children have of acting out a role.

Things To Put On

Hats of all kinds.
Make up and felt tip markers.
Belts, ties, beads, bracelets, watches.
Grown up shoes, boots, slippers.
Old clothes — smocks, shirts, raincoats.

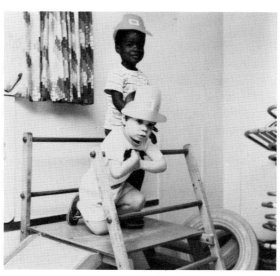

Things To Travel On

Tricycles, wagons and other wheel toys.
Cushions, medium sized boxes, or squares of cardboard.

56

Places To Go To

Large boxes
Blankets or sheets that can be thrown over a table to make a tent.
Closets.
Porches.

Things To Carry

Pocketbooks and billfolds.
Lunch boxes.
Shopping bags.
Suitcases and briefcases.

Things To Use

Toy telephone.
Keys.
Small notebook and pencil.
Bits of string and ribbons.
Dolls, stuffed animals and puppets.
Thermos bottle.
Real or toy pots, pans, dishes, utensils.
Old typewriter or cash register.
Assorted small boxes or containers.
Poker chips, small blocks.
Tongue depressors.

The producer-director needs to have a cast of characters and a set of miniature props to use with them. These materials can be provided in several ways. The child can be given a ready made playscape, a variety of miniature props or just the raw materials.

Playscapes

Playhouses, farms, doll houses, restaurants, toy villages, miniature railroads.

Miniature Type Props

Small cars, trucks and planes.
Fischer Price people, TV characters, Disney World characters, small plastic animals.

Raw Materials

Boxes and baskets.
Squares of fabric, linoleum, tile or rugs.
Blocks.
A heavy tag board or plywood square to use as a roof or floor.
Crayons, watercolors, and inexpensive paper.
Chalkboard and chalk.
Flannel board or colorform sets.

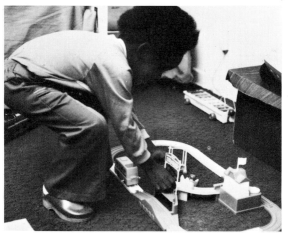

Play Space

One of the things that surprised us as we visited with different families was the number of children who had selected a special place for imaginative play. Most of the time the place was small, enclosed, and somewhat private. Frequently, it was too small for adults to get into but just right for small children. In this imaginative play spot, the real world could not intrude and the child was in control of everything that happened. Favorite places that parents mentioned were:

under the kitchen sink,
behind the sofa,
the knee hole of a desk,
under a card table with a sheet over it,
inside the fireplace,
on top of a bunk bed, and
under a toddler table.

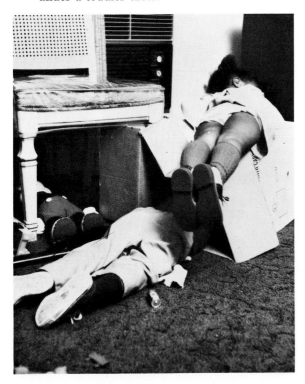

Summary

We have looked in a systematic way at the ingredients of pretend play—the interested parent, the appropriate props, the special play space. But even with these ingredients, imaginative play cannot flower without a foundation of real world experiences. The more meaningful experiences a child has the greater his potential for play. Rarely, but sadly when it happens, we see parents who substitute toys for experience. By filling the child's room with every possible toy, they develop a false sense of security about their child's development. A toy is a replication of a real world thing and if the child has not experienced the real world, he has difficulty with the analogy. Some of the important experiences for children are the everyday routine events — getting dressed, eating, cleaning up, going to the grocery store, taking a bath. Some of these experiences are the out of the ordinary events—a trip to the zoo, an airplane ride, a Thanksgiving dinner. Other important experiences come out of television, stories, and books. The importance of books as a way of expanding the child's horizons cannot be overemphasized. Many parents described their two year olds as being more interested in books than in any other play material, and the influence of books on imaginative play was evident.

Erik put a hair dryer on his head and announced that he was King Barbar. Melissa stuck a stuffed animal in her jeans and told us she was Kanga. John made a bed for Curious George to sleep in. In these examples the child is pulling out characters from books and either pretending to be the character or using the character as a companion. Occasionally, we find children incorporating some of the events from a story into their imaginative play. Francis was playing with a little yellow duck after reading a farm book with his father.

"Come on duck. Jump in the pond. Swimming in the pond. Swimming after mommy."

Although we have provided many different examples of imaginative play in this chapter, it is important to recognize that two year old children are just beginning to take advantage of the potential of pretending. Their imaginative play is not yet very sophisticated. They pack up for a trip to the beach and never leave the house. They feed the dolls a birthday cake and then blow out the candles. Most of their pretend themes are simple, and they are very dependent on parents for further elaboration.

As a matter of fact quite a few of the two's we visited were doing very little pretending. In some cases the child seemed to be busy with other developmental tasks, mastering motor skills, manipulating objects and interacting with different people. In other cases the child did not have the verbal skills to extend an imaginative play theme. But whatever the reason for this lack of pretending, it is not irreversible. With time and parent support all children can reap the benefits of imaginative play, extending the boundaries of space and time, experiencing new powers, and exploring their own creativity.

Chapter III—
Learning Through Language

    Learning To Listen 63
    Listening Activities 64
    Listening To Television 65
Reading and Listening 66
    Suggestions For Reading 68
    Teaching Two Year Olds To Read 69
    Learning To Converse 69
    Transition From Inflection To Words .. 71
    Combining Words Into Sentences 72
    Learning To Converse 73
    Affecting Another Person's Behavior .. 74
    Communicating Ideas 76
Conversational Play and Humor 79
Concluding Thought—The Role of Parents .. 80

Chapter III
Learning Through Language

No matter how often we are told that each child has his own time table of development and that it doesn't make sense to compare children, parents naturally are curious about how their child stacks up to other children. This is particularly true when it comes to language development. Brenda and her sister Phyllis each had a two and one half year old daughter. Although the cousins, Susan and Jeannette, didn't get to see each other very often, they seemed to recognize each other and enjoyed being together. One day Brenda and Phyllis were watching them play together:

> "I'm doing the farm puzzle," Jeannette announced as she struggled to fit a puzzle piece into the wrong place. "You want to do the puzzle with me? This is a hard piece — this is a very hard piece." "Me do it," Susan insisted, taking the piece out of Jeannette's hand and putting it in the puzzle. "This is my puzzle," Jeannette replied. "You can have the zoo puzzle. You like the zoo puzzle better?"
>
> "Me, me, me do," Susan insisted again and within a couple of minutes the farm puzzle was completed.

Because Brenda and Phyllis had older children, they realized that each of the cousins had her own cutting edge of development. Jeannette and Susan are both intelligent. Susan was extremely good with puzzles, although her expressive language was a bit on the slow side. Jeannette, on the other hand, talked like a three year old, but she was not as advanced with spatial relationships or small muscle tasks.

Equating language development with intelligence can lead to false conclusions. Still, most parents are concerned to some degree when language develops slowly. The burgeoning of language is the most dramatic change during the third year. In not much more than a year children go from babbling to speaking in complete sentences. Many factors influence this development. In this chapter we will discuss these factors in terms of three major aspects of language. First, we will look at how two year old children expand their ability to listen to language and to understand what it means. Second, we will explore the process of learning to speak, how children combine sounds to make words and then combine words to make sentences. Finally, we will focus on how children learn to converse with other people, how they use both their listening and speaking skills to communicate.

Each of these three sections include suggestions for enriching the language environment of two year old children. Although we know the environment has an important effect, the precise effect of any particular suggestion cannot be determined. The process of language development is not understood well enough to predict when a child will begin to talk or how fast his language will grow. However, knowing more about this process can help parents appreciate the progress that each child makes from day to day.

Learning To Listen Jason, who had just turned two, said only two words: "Dad" and "no." His parents were concerned about his language development, although in other ways he seemed normal enough. For example, he loved to explore secretly in the bathroom, unscrewing the toothpaste and squeezing it out. One day Jason's mother bought a new tube of toothpaste, but that night she could not find it. "Oh, where's that new toothpaste I bought?", she said, more to herself than to anyone else. Jason, who was standing nearby, trotted into his room and came back shortly with the toothpaste in his hand. He extended it toward his mother and smiled with the excitement and innocence characteristic of a mischievous two year old.

Although Jason shows little ability to talk, he is able to understand language. He understands common phrases like "Give me that" and "Want another bite?", but he also shows comprehension of novel sentences like his mother's question about the toothpaste.

Learning to listen, and to understand, is basic to language development. Comprehension seems to lead the way to each new step. One year old babies who are babbling already recognize the names of special people and toys. Later, when they learn to say these single words, they understand complete sentences. Between the ages of two and three, children develop the capacity to comprehend stories and explanations that are far beyond their ability to express. If a child is learning to understand language in a variety of situations, then there is much less reason to be concerned about delayed speech. If comprehension is there, speech is almost certain to follow in time.

When children seem especially slow to develop listening skills, however, parents do have grounds for concern. A general lack of comprehension indicates that a child does not see the connection between language and the rest of the world. Either the child does not grasp the fact that language is used to express meaning or the child cannot understand the relationships being expressed in language.

We cannot be sure what kind of language stimulation is best for children who are slow to develop listening skills, but we believe that the language they hear should be mature. By mature we mean fully formed sentences. One family we visited was trying to simplify the language their child heard by using a reduced form of sentences, "Give stick Eric," "No touch tree," etc. Although young children often produce sentences like this, there is no evidence that they learn language more easily by hearing such sentences.

Listening skills are ahead of speaking skills, and children want to hear language that is more complicated than the language they can produce. It is not difficult to tell when children are exposed to language that is too complex for them. They simply walk away and tune it out. On the other hand, there is no clear sign when a child is being exposed to language that is too simple. With a child whose language development is slow, parents may underestimate the child's ability and over simplify the language he hears.

It is especially difficult to be relaxed and creative in talking to a young child when the child does not seem to understand as much as you expect. So much depends on our expectations. Parents can talk easily to an infant because they do not expect much understanding — an occasional smile or gurgle is more than enough to keep them talking. As a child gets older, expectations change, and it becomes frustrating to carry on a conversation by yourself. Yet we are convinced that a child whose language development is slow needs to hear a variety of language forms just as much as other children.

Listening Activities

Let's look at some of the ways parents can stimulate listening skills. When children are just beginning to understand language, parents tend to direct them:

"Show me your bellybutton — now, where is my bellybutton?"
"Where does the orange peel go — over there in the garbage."
"Bring a book to Mommy and she'll read a story to you."

Parents use these statements to teach their children and to check on their progress in learning to understand language. Young children usually enjoy following directions and these activities may evolve into social games.

One kind of listening game that parents can initiate might be called the rhetorical question game. Stacey had recently learned to open the closet doors. Naturally she needed to practice this new ability. So whenever things got unusually quiet around the house her parents were pretty sure she was hiding in some closet. The only question was — which one? "We better go find Stacey," her mother would announce in a loud voice. "Yes, let's try our bedroom first," answered Stacey's father in an equally loud voice. "Do you think she's in the jewelry box?" asked the mother. "Probably not" replied the father, "but she might be." "Hmm...not there," mused the mother. "I know—she is in the dirty clothes hamper —Oh, no, I bet I threw her in the washing machine by mistake this morning." Long before her mother came up with this preposterous theory, Stacey's presence was made evident by her stifled giggles inside the closet. "Maybe I had better look in this closet before we go to the washing machine," suggested Stacey's father offhandedly. "Well, what do you know—here she is—in our closet." This kind of charade is marvelous stimulation for a child's language comprehension and, at the same time, it is great fun for parents to exercise their creativity.

Singing is a popular listening activity between the ages of two and three, particularly on long car trips or just before sleep time. Many parents, after singing the same song over and over till they can't stand it any more, discover that both they and their child can have a lot more fun with the song if they change the words around.

One day on a car trip Steven's father started to sing "The Bear Went Over the Mountain," mainly because he couldn't think of any other song to sing. Steven asked for more so his father began to sing about transportation, a popular topic with Steven. "The bear drove a motorcycle, the bear drove a motorcycle, the bear drove a motorcycle up to the top of the mountain." "More" said Steven. Soon the bear was driving all kinds of trucks and highway

equipment. "why just the bear?" thought Steven's father, who was getting a little bored. "The lion drove the school bus... The mouse drove a cement mixer... The giraffe came on roller skates." Steven's father was enjoying the unique traffic jam on top of the mountain.

On another day Steven's father hit upon the idea of having a party on top of the mountain. Steven was fascinated by birthday parties. "The bear said, 'Let's have a party,' the bear said, 'let's have a party,' the bear said, 'let's have a party and everyone can come.' The squirrel said, 'I'll bring some cheese cake...' the zebra said, 'I'll bring potato chips...' the gorilla said, 'I'll bring the pickles...'" for the birthday party.'"

These private songs and language games are invariably products of the moment. Parents discover them as if by chance, because they take the time to relax and let their minds take off. They instinctively know what subjects are especially important to their child, and they let their own imagination and the child's excited response be their guides. Every family and every situation offers its own opportunities. Jodi's mother discovered that Jodi liked to listen to stories in French and Spanish, even though she did not understand these languages. Brandon's mother found that he liked to lie in bed with her and listen as she read the newspaper out loud. Chad's parents invented new verses for "She'll Be Coming Round the Mountain." The "Old McDonald" that Chris knows is a mechanic—he has every kind of vehicle you can name on his farm. And so it goes.

Listening to Television

Many two year olds like to watch Sesame Street, even watching the same show twice a day, and they may have a few favorite cartoon shows, family shows, or other children's programs. Without doubt they listen to the language on these programs, but our impression is that they concentrate on processing the visual information. Television is primarily a visual medium, and the pace of information is usually very fast and full of special effects. The plots on television programs, as hackneyed as they may seem to adults, are usually too complicated for two year olds. The personal element also is missing in that television characters cannot talk spontaneously with children. All of these reasons may contribute to a lack of interest in the language of television programs.

Two year old children certainly recognize familiar faces, like Bert and Ernie. They even may recognize certain skits between the two Muppets. But the meaning of Bert and Ernie's conversation does not seem to sink in very far. The children do not ask many questions about what they hear and they do not imitate the language of the Muppets in their own speech or imaginative play.

In many of the homes we visited the television was left on while we were there. The children ignored these "adult" programs, but they were attentive to commercials. Apparently they were attracted by the catchy music, the animation, or an oversized head staring at them from the television screen. However, they also seemed to be listening to the words, the same words always following each other in a completely predictable pattern. It was a chance for them to practice their listening skills, even if the message was not relevant to them. The children were just as interested in a commercial for aspirin as they were in a toy advertisement. Parents reported that it was not until later, around the age of three, that their children began clamoring for the toys and cereals pictured in the commercials.

When children show interest in television commercials it is a sign that they would welcome listening to simple story records. These records have the same appeal as commercials—clearly articulated language, a musical background, and a short message that can be repeated over and over. The obvious difference is that the record eventually makes sense to the children. The familiar strings of words turn into meaningful sentences.

READING AND LISTENING

One of the most striking differences between the families that we visited was their use of books. It was not uncommon for parents to tell us that they spend from two to four hours every day reading to their two year old. We were amazed that parents had this much time to devote to reading. Other parents spent virtually no time reading to their children. However, even among families where it was obvious that books were seldom used, the children showed an intense interest when we began to read to them. The desire of a two year old to listen as an adult reads is an authentic phenomenon.

Toddlers are attracted to books for two reasons, the pictures and the pages. They like to look at the pictures and to practice turning the pages. By the age of two most children are interested in associating words with the pictures. Typically this association consists of naming the objects in a picture.

Two year olds continue to be interested in labeling pictures. Books especially designed for this purpose, like those by Richard Scary, are very popular. The children learn to recognize and to pronounce the names of exotic animals and specialized vehicles that they are not likely to see in the real world. However, there are numerous instances in which labeling within the simplified context of a book leads to recognition of real objects in the outside world.

Amy, at the age of 32 months, became interested in a book of signs. Her favorite sign was EXIT. To her parents' amazement she began to point out EXIT signs in restaurants and stores. Then she started noticing STOP signs, IN and OUT signs, NO signs. The sign book they read at home was clearly the inspiration for these discoveries.

Andy, when he was 34 months, liked to read a clock book. It so happened that the boy in the story had to go to bed at 8 o'clock, just like Andy. One night, as Andy was putting on his pajamas, he announced "It's 8 o'clock" and pointed to the clock. In the next few months he learned to recognize 10 o'clock, when Sesame Street came on, and 5 o'clock, the time his father came home from work. It intrigued Andy that his father started home at 5 o'clock, but did not get home until after five. When 5 o'clock came along, Andy often smiled in a satisfied manner and said, "Daddy is in his car now."

As our examples indicate, labeling may consist of more than simply attaching a name to an object. It may involve labeling a word, or a time, or a quantity. Of course, children eventually must go beyond labeling in order to read, to tell time, or to count. But labeling is a first step, and books offer a natural opportunity to see if your child is interested in taking that step.

The big leap in development occurs when children realize that there is a connection between the pages, that the pictures and words tell a story. This discovery seems to be a gradual one, like piecing together a puzzle. Each time a favorite book is read,

a bit more of the story is recognized. Erik's favorite book at two years of age was a book about a birthday party. Having recently celebrated his own birthday, it was easier for him to follow the events in the story. Reading the book both refreshed his memory and provided an imaginary party. If every day could not be his birthday, at least he could read the birthday book.

When children are first learning to follow a story they insist on hearing it over and over. As they memorize the flow of words they often object to minor editorial changes by parents. Parents get tired of this repetition, but in a surprisingly short time, two year olds become interested in a wide variety of story themes. Their powers of imagination develop to the point where they can enjoy stories about experiences they have never had, like taking a trip in a rocket, digging for gold in the desert, or having a pet kangaroo.

Most children still will have favorites, and whenever a story is connected to a special experience in their lives, that story may become a temporary obsession. Airplane trips may produce a burst of interest in airplane stories, feeding the animals on a farm can lead to a fascination with farm stories, a visit to the doctor often stimulates extra interest in stories about hospitals, etc.

When parents get too bored by this constant repetition they can try recording a story on a tape recorder. If two year old children are already familiar with a book, they are capable of listening to the story on tape and turning the pages by themselves at the right moment.

Parents can also make reading more interesting for themselves by expanding a story. Although children do not like leaving out part of a story, they often welcome adding more to it. One way to elaborate a story is to add dialogue. The pictures in most children's books include incidental characters, a squirrel in a tree or a mouse behind a rock. These characters

may play no role in the actual story, but there is no reason they cannot become involved. If Curious George crashes his bike, the squirrel who is looking on in the picture can say, "I hope George is alright," or "I wish I had a bike like that," or any number of other things. Children can create new dialogue too, once they catch on to the idea that any character can talk anytime in a story. When reading the story of the tortoise and the hare, Nicole added that the hare was sleeping because he went to bed late last night (after visiting his cousins), and that he felt sad because he had to sleep alone.

Two year old children are especially interested in stories that speak to their fears and anxieties. There are many dangers that they are not aware of at this age but certain things do worry them. They invariably are concerned about things being broken and people injured, about things being lost and people being abandoned. It is no coincidence that the Curious George stories have been so popular for over thirty years. The two year old can easily identify with a little monkey who is always making a mess, breaking important objects, getting lost, or being stuck in a cage.

Sometimes children become so involved in the imaginative experience of a story that they cannot accept one of these fearful occurrences. Kori really liked stories about a giant dog named Clifford. Clifford had a habit of rolling over and smashing things that got in his way. In one story he rolled on the family car and smashed it. Kori became quite upset and insisted, "Clifford no smash car, Clifford no smash car." The imaginative fear had become too real, and Kori had to deny that it happened. Kori's mother suggested that Clifford could fix the car. "No," replied Kori, "Clifford no have hands." Kori had become a strict realist as far as this event was concerned.

When children indicate an unwillingness to accept an imaginative experience that is too fearful, that part of the story can be skipped. Robert, like many children, was straightforward in his solution to this problem. If he did not like part of a story, he announced "The End", and slammed the book shut. Because young children cannot read for themselves, it is important to give them some degree of control over the activity. If they want to skip an objectionable page, or stop the story in the middle, or even read the story from the back to the front, parents can be accommodating.

Suggestions For Reading

Sometimes children aren't as interested in books as their parents would like. The parents complain that their children don't like to sit still, that their attention span is too short, that they won't pay attention to a story. Children do differ in their attitude toward books. However, nearly every child likes to read books on some level. Let's look at some of the ways to make early reading more fun.

First, be willing to change the words in a story if they are too complicated. Paraphrasing is not that difficult if you take your time. Read the page silently and then state in your own words what is happening. Or you can look at the pictures and describe what you see. To simplify the story, spend more time talking about the action and less time describing the scene or the inner thoughts of the characters.

Second, be aware of any responses your children make to the pictures. If they point to a certain object or say the name of a favorite character, stop your storytelling and talk briefly about that object or character, "That's right, that is Peter Rabbit—look, he has a toothbrush."

Third, let children turn the pages if they want to. You may be surprised how much this simple idea increases their involvement. They also can indicate nonverbally when they want to skip pages or discontinue the story.

Fourth, avoid turning the activity into a test. There sometimes is a fine line between a child participating in a reading activity and being put on the spot. When they read a book about animals, Nelson's father always asked Nelson questions like, "How does the pig go? How does the owl go?" Nelson was so pleased with his animal sounds that he beamed from ear to ear and clapped enthusiastically for himself. Brandon's mother liked to hesitate at the end of a sentence and let Brandon supply the last word: "The duck ... waddles. The Bear ... shuffles. The monkey ... swings." These activities are fun for both parents and children. Brandon made everyone laugh when he said that the frog "frogs." After all, the fly "flies". Yet this kind of activity can turn into a test, especially as children get older and resist performing in front of strangers. Then the reading experience will not be pleasant for either parents or children.

Teaching Two Year Olds to Read

Two year old children like to read, but there is reading and there is "reading." Jamie liked to read by pointing to the letters in a word. "M...I...L...K says milk," he announced pointing to the correct letters on the carton. His mother smiled broadly. Running over to the T.V. he continued, "Z...E...N...I...T...H says television." "Well, not exactly," his mother corrected, but she was still smiling broadly. His earnestness was impressive.

Katie was reading the story of Gingerbread Boy to her doll while Katie's mother was fixing lunch and eavesdropping. "Once-a-time there was Mommy and Daddy and Gingerbread Boy. Gingerbread Boy outside. Here comes the wolf —I want to eat Gingerbread Boy. Gingerbread Boy ran home too fast to his Mommy. And that was the end of the wolf." Katie put the doll down and laid the open book over the doll's face, "Now you read the story, I'm too busy." And she went into the kitchen to see what was for lunch.

Kim and her mother were sitting at the dining table. Kim's mother had a stack of homemade flashcards. "OK Kim, what does this word say?" "Daddy," said Kim. "Good, now what about this one?" "Ice cream." "Right — now read this word." "Cake?" "No, try again." "Candy?" "No." "Bubble gum!" "No, this is the word house! Remember you learned that a couple of weeks ago." Kim sighed and so did her mother. Reading was hard work.

Pretend reading, as illustrated by Jamie and Katie, is delightful for both parents and children. The children demonstrate a sense of accomplishment and they see reading as a pleasant activity. The parents are entertained and at the same time get new insights into the thinking process of their children. Real reading, as illustrated by Kim, tends to be a tedious business between the ages of two and three.

We were surprised by the number of parents in our study who were trying to teach their child to read. It is true that two year olds enjoy learning to recognize numbers and letters. Sesame Street, more than anything else, has called children's attention to these shapes and has increased parents' awareness that children can learn the alphabet. However, it is a long step between recognizing letters and reading. Two year olds can learn to recognize some sight words, especially words with strong emotional appeal, but they usually forget them unless there is constant repetition.

The parents in our study who had tried to accelerate reading had not met with much success. One mother reported that after a year and a half of instruction, her child could read simple three word sentences like, "I see cat." Another mother told us that her three year old daughter could read a few books, but wouldn't unless the mother read one first. "She keeps losing her place on the page," the mother noted. Results like these do not seem worth the effort.

Learning To Converse

Learning to listen may be basic to language development, but learning to speak is more significant to parents. We eagerly anticipate a child's first words and when they appear we start listening for the child's first sentences. There often is a relatively long time, six months or more, during which a child's speaking ability seems to expand very slowly. This dormant period typically occurs between one and two years of age. When it happens, parents become worried... Brenda understands almost everything we say, and she can pronounce words — why doesn't she start saying all the words she understands? ... Then one day Brenda's parents realized that her vocabulary was bursting with new words. Now she only needs to hear a word once before it is picked up.

This pattern of slow, almost non-existent vocabulary growth, followed by a rapid spurt, is not the only way children start to speak, but is is common. There probably are several reasons for this pattern, but a primary reason is that the process of articulating words is so difficult. We take for granted our ability to imitate sounds that we hear. In actuality this ability is a small miracle. We never see the tongue and palate movements that are necessary to produce each consonant and vowel, neither our own movements nor those of other speakers. Yet we translate what we hear into a sequence of movements by the tongue, lips, and palate. A word like "helicopter," for example, must be translated into eight successive positions. No wonder a child just starting to speak may say "heh" or "caw" or mumble something unintelligible.

If a two year old child's understanding of language is progressing satisfactorily, and yet the child is slow to speak, there is a good possibility that it is due to articulation problems. The other day Johnny was brought into our office because his parents were worried about his language development. He was 26 months old and according to his parents said only a handful of words. Having a small vocabulary is not especially unusual at this age, but Johnny's parents were comparing him to their friends' two year old daughter, who spoke fluently. Johnny was quite active during his visit, stacking blocks, throwing balls, and drawing on a chalkboard. It was evident that he understood many comments made to him, and yet the only word we heard was "baw" (ball).

The interesting thing was Johnny's extended use of this one word. He had received a tennis ball from a bag, and he requested another "baw." When one was given to him, he dropped it immediately and asked again. Soon we realized that he was not interested in another ball, but in seeing what other toys were in the bag. He was using "baw" to mean toy. Later he wanted his bottle. This time he said "baw-aw," adding a barely distinguishable syllable to his usual uterance. At the end of the interview we concluded that Johnny spoke little because he had not yet learned to articulate many sounds. He understood language, and he certainly wanted to talk. In fact, he was doing as much as could be expected with the few sounds he did control.

Usually children solve these articulation problems by themselves in a few months and rapidly catch up in speaking skills. We do not know why some young children master the basic rules of articulation more quickly than others or why some children pronounce their words much more clearly than others. In any event, articulation skills are not fully developed until the age of eight. Parents sometimes think that if two year old children have minor articulation problems, they will have them for the rest of their lives. This is not the case, and speech therapy is not appropriate.

Young children often practice articulation skills by imitating the last word or last syllable of sentences they hear. When we went to visit Brian, who was 32 months old, his mother told us he did not talk much. Yet we heard him repeating to himself the last word in his mother's sentences: "Here, Brian, eat your popsicle" ... "sicle." "Oh, now you got yourself all sticky" ... "icky." His attempts to imitate language were ignored by his mother and grandmother. At the same time, they punished him when he tried to imitate adults in other ways. He was slapped on the hand for feeding the dog, turning on the electric typewriter, or giving his baby sister a cookie. Instead of blossoming, Brian's imitative behavior seemed stuck on a primitive level and was leading to intense conflict within the family. Brian's case suggests that rejecting a child's attempts to imitate may delay speech.

The best way to encourage young children to improve their articulation is to give them opportunities to talk to a wide range of people. Gillian used to talk on the telephone every day to her father at the office. Some other people in the office wanted to say "hello" too. Gillian usually called right after lunch, and often she reported on the food she did not like. "I no like cely," she announced one day. "You don't like jelly?" the secretary asked. "No, no," said Gillian, "I no like *cely*." "I don't understand you, Gillian," answered the secretary. "Soup," Gillian explained. Although the secretary never did figure out that Gillian meant celery soup, our example illustrates the process by which misunderstanding creates pressure for better articulation.

In families where there are twins parents often complain about delayed speech. This apparent delay may indicate a language difference rather than a language problem. Often twins have invented their own words for things. Sometimes this private language is not shared with the rest of the family, and parents find themselves in the position of learning a language as they try to figure out what all the funny invented words mean. Chris and Michael, who had just turned two, were playing some sort of game with blocks and a plastic bird. We caught an occasional syllable. "Too too," said Michael as he lifted his block to his ear. Chris' reply was mostly unintelligible except for "bee bee" and "bye bye." Their mother couldn't figure out what the game was about either but she did translate some words — "too too" meant telephone, "bye bye" was peanut butter and "bee bee" was Birdie. Do you suppose Christopher was ordering peanut butter for his plastic bird?

The Transition From Inflection To Words

Talking is a matter of inflection as well as words. Inflection is the music of speech, the pitch and tone of voice and the rhythm of phrases. Babies are more attentive to inflection than to words. When spoken in a horrified tone of voice, a word like "hot" communicates a sense of danger to a baby long before he understands the specific meaning of the word. Between the ages of one and two, many children demonstrate an amazing control of inflection. They chatter away in their own foreign tongue using familiar inflection patterns or as it is called "expressive jargon." Therefore, their language sounds real to us, even though we cannot identify any real words.

Toddlers use their control of inflection to communicate. They send inflectional messages — "I'm happy, I'm angry, I want more food, I want out of my crib, I want to be carried." Using words to communicate represents a new strategy, and some children seem to be unwilling to give up the old style that parents already understand.

April had mastered every detail of the daily schedule in her family, and she was clever at getting what she wanted. If she wanted to hear a story, she would hand a book to her mother, make an excited, pleading sound, and then clap her hands. April's mother knew the routine was manipulative but it was so cute. April's father, on the other hand, responded well when April stamped her little foot and made a menacing sound with her voice. He found this "fierce" behavior quite charming.

April was only 24 months old, and her parents were not concerned about the fact that she used few words. In the future, however, they are likely to find her inflectional messages less appealing. They will expect April to change her strategy for communicating, to use words primarily and inflection secondarily.

Parents in this kind of situation may subscribe to the "lazy tongue" theory. Essentially this theory is as follows: If children understand language, and they can pronounce a few words clearly, the reason they do not talk more is that they are lazy. They will not make the effort to say a word when a grunt, a squeal, or a gesture will work instead. According to this theory, the solution to the problem lies in making sure that laziness is not rewarded. Parents are advised to stop responding to a child's inflectional messages. If the child wants a drink of milk, make him say the word "milk" before you give it to him. Stop coddling the child and force him to use language.

From our perspective, learning to talk is an extremely complex and difficult task. If some children are slow to speak, it is simplistic to assume that it is caused by laziness. Moreover, we doubt very much the efficacy of forcing children to communicate. Imagine you were in a foreign language class 24 hours a day, and you could not watch your favorite television program, eat your favorite desserts, read your favorite magazines, or call your favorite friends until you could pronounce certain words in the foreign language. Given the circumstances, you might very well learn these words, but what would be your attitude toward the instructor? Would you feel like communicating with him? Those who survived and succeeded in such a foreign language class would feel justifiably proud of their accomplishment, but there also would be numerous dropouts. We suspect the same kind of process happens with young children. Forcing children to talk will cause many to withdraw even more.

One of the ways to recognize the ingredients of a facilitative environment is to look at the families in which children talk early. We invariably find parents who are very sensitive to their child's tone of voice and mood. These parents respond to any messages their children send, whether they are based on words, inflection or gesture.

Jennifer, at one year old, had developed a pointing game. As soon as her mother picked her up, she pointed to a window or picture across the room. She expected her mother to go over there and talk about what she was seeing.

"Look, Jennifer, there's a bird out in the tree. Isn't she a pretty bird?"
"Da, da," (Jennifer).
"That's right, there is some dirt on the window."
"Da, da," (Jennifer).
"Oh, you want down? OK."
"Da, da," (Jennifer).

"Oh, I see what you got — your duck."
"Da, da," (Jennifer).
"Yes, the duck is like the bird in the tree. Very good."

Jennifer's mother discovered a multitude of messages in Jennifer's "Da, da." Perhaps some of these messages were not even there — it does not really matter. The important thing is her mother's orientation. She assumes that the more she responds to Jennifer's messages, no matter how ill-formed, the more messages Jennifer will send. In our experiences this is exactly what happens. Jennifer's mother usually responds with some verbalization. Even when she is granting a request, such as putting Jennifer down, she describes the action. By modeling a variety of messages, she undoubtedly helps Jennifer learn to formulate her own.

Jennifer still is using inflection and gesture as her primary means of communication. At some point she may need to abandon this strategy in favor of words. In Jennifer's case we can predict this transfer will be accomplished easily, so easily in fact that her parents may never notice it. Jennifer will find the change easy because she has so many different messages to send. She will not be satisfied much longer to point in the general direction she wants her mother to go. She will start pointing at specific objects, wanting to hold them and wanting her mother to talk about them. Pointing to the cupboard when she is hungry will be even less satisfactory. She may get a cracker when she wants the honey. As the specificity of her messages increases, so will her incentive to use words.

We do not want to imply that when children are slow to talk, it necessarily means that their parents are unresponsive. There are a number of possible reasons for delayed speech. Our point is that trying to force children to talk is not a particularly effective way to develop language. We recommend trying to expand the number and variety of messages children want to send. Parents can encourage this variety by pointing out interesting sights, by describing their children's actions, by playing listening games, and by reading books. We believe that if children want to communicate a variety of messages, they eventually will find that words are necessary.

Combining Words Into Sentences

Once children begin to use a large variety of one-word messages, it is only a matter of a few weeks or months before the words are combined into sentences. Some children go through a stage of two-word sentences, followed by three and then four-word sentences, systematically building their grammatical expertise. Other children use familiar phrases and simple sentence frames from the start. The progression from one to several words is impressive enough, but the grammatical elaboration that soon follows is truly astounding. After six months to a year of talking in sentences, children have acquired the basic grammar of English.

This feat is accomplished without any direct instruction from adults. Children listen to the language around them and come up with their own rules of grammar. Imitation plays a part in that children pick up the phrases and vocabulary of their parents, but they have their own system for creating sentences.

We know young children have their own rules of grammar because they systematically make mistakes that they have never heard. For example, a two year old may say, "me going store," instead of "I going store." The children have never heard anyone else use "me" like this. However, they have learned from listening that "me" is used as a self-reference and, therefore, they use it in all cases. We might say they have learned only part of the rule in standard English.

The grammar of children is sometimes more logical than the grammar of their parents because the children have not learned that every rule has exceptions. For example, when children learn to form plurals by adding an "s," they change foot to foots or feets. When they learn to form the past tense by adding "ed," they change go to goed, or hit to hitted.

Between the ages of two and three, children learn to fill in the little words that are missing in their earlier sentences. "Me going Mama store," becomes "I am going with my Mama to the store." Words like "the, with, my," and "to," are not usually necessary to understand simple sentences, but they specify the meaning more precisely. One day parents suddenly realize that their children are routinely inserting common prepositions and adjectives into sentences.

There are two kinds of sentences that are especially difficult to construct, although both are common. These sentences are questions and negative statements. Their combination, a negative question, is even harder. Parents can watch their two year olds progressing step by step with these sentences. One of the first steps in forming questions is to learn special question words that can be placed at the beginning of a sentence: "Why you fixing my tricycle?" "Where you going?" A second step, which often does not begin to appear until the age of three, is to use the direct helping verb at the beginning of the question: "Why *are* you fixing my tricycle?" "Where *are* we going?" The development of negative sentences is somewhat similar. At first children learn to add a negative word to the sentence: "I no like dogs." "I not going home." Later they begin to add the appropriate helping verb: "I *am* not going home." "I *do* not like dogs."

We have greatly oversimplified the complexities of questions and negative sentences. Most three year olds have only begun the process of learning these rules. Several more years of listening and talking will be needed before they are fully understood. The best way to help children develop grammatical competence is to expose them to many examples of proper grammar and to encourage them to express themselves as much as possible. As we emphasized with articulation, it is conversation and not instruction that is the key to language development.

Two year old children also practice their grammar by talking to themselves. Typically, these monologues occur when children are quietly occupied, going to sleep, playing in the bathtub, or riding in a car. A child may start with a simple phrase and build it up into a more complex one: "Bye-bye Nana. Have a nice time Nana. Have a nice time at school Nana. Have a nice time working on papers Nana." The reverse exercise may occur, breaking a long phrase down into a simple one. Sometimes children invent substitute exercises: "riding on a camel, riding on a boat, riding on a plane," or they practice making negative statements, "the car's too hot—not too hot; it's too far—not too far." Other drills may involve pronouns, pluralization, or any other grammatical rules children incorporate into their language at this age. The desire of children to master the rules of grammar is an amazing phenomenon.

Learning To Converse

Billy: "I want catsup."
Mother: "Don't you remember, you broke it yesterday?"
Billy: "We buy more catsup at store?"
Mother: "Sure, next time we go. How about mustard for your sandwich?"
Billy: "This mustard bites my mouth."
Mother: "Here, let's mix it with some mayonnaise."
Billy: "I don't like mayonnaise."

Mother: "Sure you do. You always eat it with salami."
Billy: "This is not salami. It's olive loaf."
Mother: "Well, it's the same thing really. Anyway, this isn't mayonnaise — it's mustardaise."
Billy: "Yea, mustardaise. No catsupaise — just mustardaise."
Mother: "And it will make your ears grow."

A conversation is both an exchange of information and a social interaction. Within the back and forth rhythm we can see that Billy has developed considerable conversational skill. He can form questions, arguments, comments, and even a joke. Like many conversations with two year olds, Billy's primary purpose in this exchange is to get adult help. He wants some improvement in his sandwich, and he uses language to affect his mother's behavior. Although the conversation does not focus on new information, several ideas are communicated. Catsup comes from stores, mayonnaise cuts the strong taste of mustard, and olive loaf is like salami. There also is a playful aspect to this conversation. Billy argues only half-heartedly about the mayonnaise, and when his mother invents a new term, he plays with it and comes up with his own new word. Using language to affect another person's behavior, using language to communicate ideas, and using language just for fun — we will discuss each of these functions in turn, although in real conversations they often are inseparably intermingled.

Affecting Another Person's Behavior

From an early age children use language to make their wishes known. Between the ages of two and three they learn to back up these desires and requests with arguments. The "No" of the toddler gives way to more sophisticated forms of self-assertion. As Kori put it when she was told to go inside, "I am Myla Kori Bardige, and I'm not going inside." Loosely translated, this argument seems to be; "I am an important person and, therefore, when I say no, it carries weight."

There is a strong imitative element in these early arguments. When Kori's mother meant business, she used Kori's full name, and Kori was imitating this practice. Even when this imitative language is directed at parents in anger, it usually is easy to tolerate because it is so entertaining. Brad informed his mother, "You drive me up a wall," when he was told to take a nap, and Erik snorted, "fridiculous" when told to put on his coat before going outside.

Two year olds go beyond using imitative language to contradict their parents. They also turn parents' arguments back on them. Lisa liked to answer the phone, and she resisted giving the phone to her mother by saying, "You don't know them."

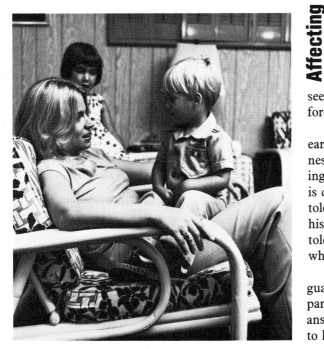

Randy refused to eat his dinner because "I'm a baby and babies don't have to eat dinner." Matthew told his father, "You have to share your tools with me cause I share my tools with you."

When children use the phrases and arguments of their parents, they may not successfully control their parents' behavior, but at least some of the tension surrounding the conversation is released. Sometimes parents laugh and agree with the child's point of view; sometimes they insist on their own perspective, but in a gentler tone of voice. Although the arguments of two year old children often make us smile, we should remember that they are serious. Children do fot argue with us in order to be amusing but in order to make a point. Sooner or later they will push their arguments far enough to annoy us or even make us angry.

It was funny the first time Patty said she was "too busy" to put on her clothes. After being late to nursery school every day for two weeks, however, the situation was different. Stephanie's mother smiled when Stephanie said she was "not perky" and needed another vitamin pill. But Stephanie could not be convinced that one was enough, and she turned breakfast into a tense time by continually whining, "I need more."

Probably the most difficult kind of argument to handle is being told to be quiet. Jon told his parents to stop reminding him about the toilet by saying, "I want done that." Other children are even more direct. They cut parents off in the middle of their lectures by saying, "No talk," or "Go away." These responses are infuriating to parents who already are inflamed enough.

On the one hand it is unrealistic to anticipate laughing off every argument that a two year old formulates. On the other hand, it does not make much sense to go to the other extreme and always punish a two year old for arguing, or "talking back." The most primitive and least flexible way to exercise control in a conversation is to force the conversation to end, and this is what we do when we do not allow children to argue with us. The ability of two year old children to argue follows naturally from their growing conversational skill. If we refuse to let children argue with us, we are encouraging them to drop out of future conversations by ignoring us. They may appear to be more polite, but what they are really doing is paying less attention to us.

Many arguments with two year old children cannot be resolved satisfactorily because the children do not understand the concepts involved in the argument. For example, when Terry's parents told him that he needed to go to bed in order to rest, he insisted that he was not tired. Indeed his energy level was very high because he speeded up when he got tired. Telling Terry that he needed rest because he would be very busy the next day, or after his nap, was no good either. He could not understand the relationship between rest and energy, and his ability to project himself into the future was quite imprecise. Terry's parents realized that he did not understand their explanations, but they still allowed Terry to argue with them. They accepted Terry's feeling that this issue was an important topic for conversation.

The more young children argue, the better they become at it and the more likely they are to gain a compromise. At some point every parent reaches a limit and refuses to argue about a subject any more. But until that point is reached, two year old children are learning about a valuable aspect of conversation, the fine art of negotiation and compromise.

When compromise is not possible, children may opt for saving face. One day Stacy did not like what the family was having for dinner. "I want a hot dog," she told her mother. "I'm sorry, we don't have any," was the reply. Stacy consoled herself by saying, "Maybe tomorrow." Her mother doubted that hot dogs would be served the next day, but she let the comment pass, knowing that by tomorrow Stacy would have forgotten about it. Beverly's attempt to save face was even more transparent. She was denied dessert because she had not eaten her dinner, and as the rest of the family ate their ice cream, she rationalized, "I don't like ice cream anyway." Having the last word is a pyrrhic victory, but it often is sufficient for the two year old child. Not able to control the situation, they at least can control the conversation.

Questions certainly can be used to affect the behavior of another person, and two year old children sometimes ask for things they want. However, they are more apt to state their wishes as commands. Questions serve another purpose. They can be used to control and to extend a conversation. As children learn to form questions, they explore the potential of this new power. For example, many two year old children pester their parents by asking, "What's this?" when they already know the answer. Another popular question is "What you doing?" which can be used in any situation to start a conversation. The overuse of "why" questions is the most noticeable of all. Asking "why" usually is an effective way to keep a conversation going. Of course, if children ask too many "why" questions, conversation breaks down altogether. Jennifer, a three year old, ended up answering her own questions, "Why is that—I know, I know because God made it that way."

Conversations with children who have just turned two are likely to be pretty one-sided affairs. Parents are in control of the conversation, asking all the questions, and answering most of them as well. Although young two year olds can make their wishes known, they are limited to simple resistance if a confrontation develops. A year later the situation has changed dramatically. The children are able to argue surprisingly well with their parents, and in many conversations they ask most of the questions. Conversations are genuine back and forth exchanges, with both parents and children using language to affect the behavior of each other.

Communicating Ideas

"You're dynamite," Zacky said happily to his mother. "I go to potty once, no kidding," Chris promised his father. "I don't need this aggravation," yelled Chad at a frustrating toy. Examples like these show how sophisticated two year old children can sound when they use the language of their parents to communicate ideas. More often, however, they use their own words to communicate information and their sentences sound more child like.

Probably the most typical kind of information two year old children try to communicate is a description of what they see. Evan, who was just two, pointed out every McDonald's that the family passed. Lisa, at two and one half, concentrated on finding Pizza Huts. Laura, a three year old, noticed McDonald's, Burger King, Pizza Hut, International Pancake House, Kentucky Fried Chicken, and Denny's.

Whether it is restaurants, or trucks, or animals, or any other category of objects that is especially interesting to two year old children, we see a similar pattern. Children start with a particular favorite and look for it everywhere in their environment. The idea they are communicating is, "There is another one of those interesting things called . . ." After days or weeks of exhaustive searching, they often switch to a new favorite. Gradually the category expands and the observational skills of the children become more flexible. They watch for, and comment on, a variety of favorites.

Stating the name of an object represents a minimal description. Between two and three, children learn to describe what they see in more detail. Negative characteristics are frequently prominent in these descriptions. Things are messy, greasy, dirty, stinky, broken, slippery, lost, tricky, etc. However, children at this age are also interested in talking about more objective attributes of objects, such as color and size.

Brian said, "red" whenever the family stopped at a traffic light, and then he yelled, "green" as soon as the light changed. Stacy learned the color orange by looking for Union 76 signs. Colors, like other categories, are seldom learned all at once. Children start with one or two favorite colors, then switch to other favorites, and after a year or more of trial and error, the whole spectrum has been distinguished.

Size terms form a different pattern. They come in opposites. Kathy received a little chair on her second birthday. For several months after that she always brought the chair into the living room when visitors came and compared her "little" chair to her father's "big" chair. "Big" and "little" (or tiny) stand out for almost all two year olds. However, many other opposite terms are common also—tall-short, good-bad, easy-hard, first-last, slow-fast, up-down, in-out, hot-cold, loud-quiet, pretty-ugly. The precise terms that children learn depend on the language they hear and the objects that interest them.

Children often learn one term first in a pair of opposites. Andy learned "loud" before "quiet" because the large trucks on the highway frightened him when they passed the car. However, Erik learned "quiet" first because his mother urged him to "be quiet and take a nap." Eventually both terms in a pair of opposites are learned, and then, like Kathy and the chairs, children tend to juxtapose opposites in the same conversation. "This is slow," said Jeffrey, pushing his toy cement truck. By way of contrast he picked up a race car and said, "This is fast." Then he skimmed the race car across the floor and watched it bounce off a wall.

Opposite games may evolve. Patti and her father played a game with a large cardboard box. Patti's father dropped playing cards through a slot, while Patti, who was inside the box, pushed the cards back out: "In goes a nine—out goes a king." "In goes a two—out goes a three." Sitting in his high chair, Erik looked at his legs and stretched them out in front of him: "Now I'm tall." Tucking his legs back under the chair he said, "Now I'm short."

In describing the world around them, there are two little words that many young children find especially useful—"too" and "like." Toys are "too high" to reach; puzzles are "too hard"; clothes are "too big" or "too small"; there are "too many bugs" or "too much snow." "Too is an ideal word for expressing feelings of frustration over an excess in the state of things. "Like," which is another very flexible term, is ideal for talking about similarities. A pickle can look "like an alligator"; the moon can look "like a banana"; a football game on T.V. can look "like Wheaties." When "too" and "like" appear in the descriptions of children, a new level of subtlety is possible. It is interesting for parents to observe the kind of excesses and similarities that their children comment on.

Probably the most fascinating thing about the descriptive statements of young children is their ability to use words in new ways. Robert did not have a word to convey his dislike of cherries and grapes in fruit cocktail, so he referred to them as "dirty." They were a kind of dirt in his dessert. Erik did not have a word to describe the jumble of toys he had created on the floor, so he called it "a big traffic jam." Kristin called her mother's bra "a white nipple." Ian packed his case suit. Heather served cake cream at her pretend birthday party. Raymond told the doctor that he didn't want a bleeding. This kind of word creativity gives us another indication of the contrasts and analogies that children see around them.

In many conversations that focus on the communication of ideas, two year old children take the role of asking questions. Although questions are used to tease parents or simply to extend a conversation, two year olds also use questions to solicit information. "What's that?" may be a genuine question, when a child sees an unusual object and wants to know its name. Another early question is "where," and some very interesting "where" questions may appear as children become more aware of disappearing objects. Christopher asked where the sun was at night. Phyllis, who was watching her shadow as she walked, wondered where the shadow went when she stood in the shade. Mark asked where a balloon was after it popped. Clarence asked where Big Bird went when the TV lost its picture. Matthew asked where the soapsuds went as they dribbled down the drain.

"Why" questions are a new development between two and three, and, as we stated earlier, it often takes a while for children to grasp the meaning of "why." Once they learn to use this question form appropriately, they tend to ask about the purpose or intention behind events: "Why you spank the cat?", "Why you painting house?"

Accidents are particularly hard to explain. Kelly asked her mother several times a day for a week, "Why Daddy drop peanut butter?" With less patience each time, her mother explained that it had been an accident, the peanut butter had slipped, Daddy wasn't using both hands, etc. Kelly found these explanations unsatisfactory because they did not specify an intention or a purpose. Breaking the peanut butter jar was not an intentional act, and neither did it serve any purpose. So Kelly remained confused as to why it had happened, and she kept asking for clarification.

Another new question form between the ages of two and three is "who?" Children discover that every person has a name. Naturally they expect their parents to know these names, just as they know the names of objects. A child may ask for the name of the mailman or the trash collector, the clerks in stores, other passengers in an elevator, or even for the names of people driving by in cars.

Although two year olds usually do not ask many "when" questions, they use other questions to find out about time sequences; "What we do after nap?" "We go swimming today?" "Sesame Street on T.V.?" After enough conversations of this kind, the children pick up a standard form for expressing simple temporal relationships. These statements still have the tone of questions: "After I take a nap, then we go to restaurant?" "First we go to Grandma's house, then we go shopping?"

The ability of young children to express sequential information is limited, but they show a great desire to talk about the past. Parents find themselves describing the events of the day to their two year olds as they go to sleep at night. This routine starts innocently enough, for it is natural to remind children of a pleasant experience before they drift off to sleep. However, the intense interest of many children in these reminiscences leads to more and more detailed conversations.

Extended conversation about any topic leads away from the immediate time and place. Having just begun to communicate in sentences, two year olds are eager to explore this transcendant quality of language. Their capacity to appreciate remote times and places may be somewhat limited. The place they describe may be the neighborhood drug store and the time may be earlier that day. Their memory may seem rigid, almost mechanical, to us. Every time Halloween was mentioned Jeffrey said, "Remember the spider?" referring to an impressive Halloween display he had seen at the grocery store. Yet he continued to listen intently to his mother's recollection of putting on his costume, trick or treating, etc.

Some parents instinctively relate present experiences to past ones. "Remember" is one of their favorite words. Other parents do not talk to two year olds in this way. It is our impression that nearly all two year old children welcome this kind of conversation. The recent past holds the same fascination as a story book, for in reality each child's daily activities make up his own life story.

The parent's role is just as important in other conversations that involve the communication of ideas. The questions of two year old children are often poorly formed, and close listening is required to find out what the children are really curious about. It also takes considerable time and effort to answer the questions in a way that young children can understand. Descriptive comparisons and analogies by two year olds are usually brief, and parents need to expand them in order to sustain the conversation. The children are interested in talking about what they see, but their verbal ability lags behind their ability to observe similarities and differences. Whether a conversation consists primarily of descriptive comments, a question and answer

exchange, or a reminiscence of past experience, it is up to parents to keep the ideas flowing back and forth.

CONVERSATIONAL PLAY AND HUMOR

One of the functions of language at every age is play. the toddler who babbles happily as he removes books from the bookcase is bubbling over with good cheer. He is not trying to control or communicate, just to celebrate his mood with some verbal music. More and more of this music is set to words as the language of children matures. The two year old who is dunking her doll in the bathtub repeats to herself in a sing-song chant — "in and out — in and out." Almost every monologue has elements of playful poetry, even if its primary purpose is to guide or clarify the child's activity. As Lynn drew a picture she murmured, "Where did my chalk go? I am making a nice circle here. Where the sponge, hon? Here's the sponge, hon."

The appearance of verbal humor is a new development between the ages of two and three. As children come to understand the sense of language, they see the humor in nonsense. Nouns predominate in the early language of children, and therefore noun nonsense predominates in early humor. Again, listening precedes talking. Children understand noun jokes before they tell their own.

Michael gave his mother a double take the first time she asked him if he wanted some more "flibber." She had a dish of noodles in her hand — "was this some kind of trick," he wondered. "Do you want some more blibber? — or is it blubber?" "No," roared Michael, "just noodles," and he grabbed the dish. The broad smile on his face showed that he had understood the joke, though, and was waiting for some more of this crazy talk.

Noun nonsense evolves naturally from nursery rhymes that children have memorized. "Mary had a little elephant," recited Chad's mother, as Chad giggled quietly. Robert, who didn't like sad endings anyway, was much happier when the last little piggy went to the Pizza Hut instead of home.

Another natural opportunity to introduce humor arises when two year old children start the game of "what's this?" After dinner every night Brad insisted that his father sit down and look at a Richard Scary book with him. "What's this," Brad asked, pointing to a picture of a fried egg. "Why, that's a fried floozle," said his father. "No, silly, that's a egg."

Of course, the unparalleled master of noun nonsense is Dr. Seuss. His stories are sometimes too complicated for two year old children to follow, but they enjoy listening to the word concoctions. A particular phrase may be picked up and become part of a daily game. For example, Andy liked the phrase "a wocket in your pocket," so his parents amused him with similar questions, "Is there a wup in your cup?" "Is there a wub in the tub?"

Two year old children also are beginning to enjoy the humor of mispronounciation. Chad quickly picked up his parents' night-time routine of asking him, "Are you thoisty?" In Sherri's family everyone gets a "hugarooni," which sounds a lot more special than the usual hug. Families make up strange and humorous pet names for each other, such as "Weenie Brandini" for the more pedestrian "Brandi," or "Jody Pody," and "Sherry Cherrie."

The attempts of two year old children to produce noun jokes are usually not very funny by adult standards, but they try so hard we have to smile anyway. Beverly announced one day that "Grandma is a baby" and that "Sasha (the dog) is a kitty cat." The nonsense element is too obvious to surprise us. However, a child occasionally will hit on an unsuspected association. Michael, who demonstrates an unusual ability to rhyme at this age, called his mother Lisa Pizza, his father Scary Larry, and his grandmother, Nana Banana.

In describing the humor that parents and two year old children share, we do not mean to suggest that there is a constant atmosphere of hilarity. Humor provides the accent to conversation, the spice. A steady diet of it soon becomes tedious for everyone. Moreover, a sense of verbal humor is just beginning to develop in children between the ages of two and three. Adults take the lead in introducing funny ideas. During the next few years the children's attempts to be funny will increase greatly as they learn to participate in the give and take of verbal humor.

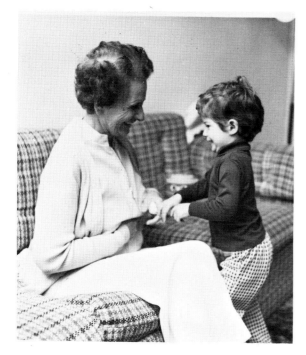

Usually there is an element of teasing in verbal humor and the distinction between being playful versus being cruel can become blurred. A child may feel belittled, rather than amused, by adult antics. More common at this age is a feeling of confusion. As Michelle put it when her mother used nonsense words, "talk nice."

On the other hand, parents may become upset with the over exuberant silliness of children, especially if it is interpreted as show off behavior. When we visited Janet, she wanted to read a book. The story consisted of animals talking about themselves. For example, on one page the bee said, "God helps me make honey." Janet teased her father by saying, "Me?" knowing full well that it was not she who made honey. This routine was repeated on every page, and when it did not sufficiently amuse her father or us, Janet began to pretend to eat the pictures, saying things like, "I'm eating grass." In this case neither Janet's father nor we were upset with Janet's determined effort to assume the center of the stage, for this was the purpose of our visit. However, on another occasion her verbal humor might have been less welcome.

CONCLUDING THOUGHT THE ROLE OF PARENTS

Language development between the ages of two and three brings out the teacher in most parents. It is a subject they feel confident in teaching, having been successful speakers for many years, and the rapid growth in the language of children demonstrates that their pupils are eager and intelligent. Very often the teacher-parent trains the pupil-child to do some language tricks. Teacher, "What does Ronald McDonald say?" Pupil: "We do it all for you ... oou." Most parents sense that these tricks are peripheral to the main stream of language development. They are the frosting on the cake.

Occasionally, however, the tricks assume more importance than they deserve. Parents become overly concerned about teaching children to speak courteously or to pronounce words properly or to read flash cards. In one family where we felt such a pattern existed the mother proudly asked her two and a half year old daughter to recite her full name, address, and telephone number. The little girl dutifully rattled off a reasonable approximation of the correct words, but obviously with almost no comprehension of their meaning. In itself there is nothing wrong with teaching a young child her address and telephone number, even if she does not understand what she is talking about. What is disturbing is the narrow view of language development that may lie behind this practice. As we have mentioned several times throughout this chapter, language is a live and spontaneous process in which parents and children can express their feelings to each other and explore the world together. It is not a bag of tricks handed down from one generation to the next.

Many parents do a splendid job of stimulating their two year old's language. They converse freely with their children, answering both questions and complaints. They read many books with their children in a way that is both informative and entertaining. However, even these parents, we feel, could often benefit from loosening up their role as language teacher.

One conscientious mother we visited had been playing with her son in a pretend situation before we arrived. He was pretending that a set of plastic rings were various fish. "Find me the biggest fish," the mother requested. "No, that's not the biggest fish," the mother continued. The biggest one is right behind you. How many fish am I holding in my hand now?" Although this mother was taking advantage of an imaginative play situation to extend her child's vocabulary she was missing the real fun of conversation. Fortunately, later in the day this same mother resumed the fish game with her son. This time she was not playing teacher.

Mother: "Thank you for finding me the little fish. I will hide him under the rock so the big fish will not scare him."
Child: "Big fish scaring him. Big fish swimming-swimming-swimming."
Mother: "Be careful, big fish—you may get stuck under the rock."
Child: "Big fish swimming under the rock. Be careful swimming under the rock.'

In the second episode, both the parent and the child were having a good time. This kind of conversation interchange combines instruction with fun.

Part 2: Social Competence

Chapter IV—Everyday Living 85
Ways of Avoiding Conflict 88
   Planning ahead and setting rules 88
   Distraction 88
   No contest 90
Ways of Resolving Conflicts 91
   Explanation 91
   Rewards 91
   Punishment 91
Daily Routines 94
   Eating 94
   Meal-time problems 94
   Eating out 96
Snacks 97
Dressing 99
Washing Up 101
Housework 102
Toilet Training 104
Sleep Time 105
Summary 107

Chapter VI—Increased Awareness 131
Self-Awareness 133
Relating To Others 137
   Within the Family 137
   Beyond the Immediate Family 141
New Discoveries 143
   Space, time and number 143
   New ideas about life 145
Summary 148
                                      131

Chapter V—Making Friends 108
Playing with Siblings 111
   Adjusting to a new baby 111
   Keeping up with older siblings 113
   Ways of responding to siblings 115
   Twins a special case 117
Playing With Friends 118
   Having an older friend 118
   Playing with another two-year-old 120
Styles of Playing 122
Group Experience 125
   Choosing the right setting 125
   A case study 126

Chapter IV — Everyday Living

Ways of Avoiding Conflict 88
    Planning ahead and setting rules 88
    Distraction 88
    No contest 90
Ways of Resolving Conflicts 91
    Explanation 91
    Rewards 91
    Punishment 91
Daily Routines 94
    Eating 94
    Meal-time problems 94
    Eating out 96
Snacks 97
Dressing 99
Washing Up 101
Housework 102
Toilet Training 104
Sleep Time 105
Summary 107

Chapter I
Everyday Living

After the third story, the fourth good night kiss, and the second glass of water, Karen's mother threw herself down on the living room sofa muttering to her husband, "She's the worst part and the best part of every day of my life." The sentiment that Karen's mother expressed is shared by many of our parents. Whether they describe their two year olds as fantastic or impossible, they always add a "but" or an "except."

"Peter is the most hard-headed kid in the world but he's so much fun to live with."

"Jessica is the ideal child except when we suggest bed time."

"Andrea is the most mild mannered of all my kids, but she's a holy terror at meal times."

Most of the negative attributes that parents complain about center around daily routines. But while routines may be the major source of all evil, they are also the source of some of the greatest pleasures of parenting. Many parents report that shared cleaning up and fixing up activities, meal time conversations, and before bed cuddle time are "the best part" of their day.

It is not surprising that daily routines give rise to heightened emotions in both parents and children. Two year olds are learning to assert their autonomy. Billy, for example, was in the habit of saying "no" to most of his parents' requests. His mother related an incident in which he insisted on putting his jacket on when the whole family was standing on one leg waiting. Then at bed time when asked to pull his shirt off, he demanded that "mommy do." Eventually all parents are placed in a position where they must exercise authority. This is not necessarily a negative outcome. Conflict situations provide parents with an opportunity to establish sensible rules, to set limits, to teach values and to help children make appropriate decisions.

From our talks with different families about the kinds of concerns they had over routines, we were able to make two rather broad generalizations. First, we recognized that the situations that brought about conflict reflected the value system of the family. Parents who were particularly concerned about nutrition were likely to have conflicts around food. Parents who were concerned with teaching independence had confrontations over dressing, toileting, or going to sleep at night.

Second, we recognized that each family had a distinctive style for meeting conflict. Despite a bewildering variety of situations, there was a pattern of consistency in the way routine problems were handled. Each family's style was a unique blend of strategies and techniques. We have categorized these techniques under two general headings: (1) ways of avoiding conflict, and (2) ways of resolving conflict.

WAYS OF AVOIDING CONFLICT

Planning Ahead and Setting Rules Andy was particularly fond of a pair of overalls with two pockets that he had inherited from his older brother. Most of the time his mother was perfectly happy to wash it at night and let him wear it in the morning, but there were exceptions. Easter morning was one of those exceptions, and Mrs. G. was not about to let him go to church with tattered overalls. The night before Easter, with the overalls still in the wash, she suggested to Andy that they go to his closet and choose an outfit for church. Andy took a while to decide between the blue pants and the green pants but finally made his decision.

Planning ahead clearly is impossible much of the time because the future is unpredictable. Some parents also complain that their two year old children become restless when told what is coming. If the children anticipate a pleasant experience they cannot wait, and if they dread the experience they stew about it. Despite these limitations, planning with a two year old is an excellent way to avoid conflict in many situations.

Planning ahead is facilitated by setting up rules that two year olds can learn and follow. In this way the daily routine becomes predictable and children can act accordingly. Children as young as two years old are capable of obeying a rule if it is stated clearly and firmly.

"No walking in the road."

"No cookies in the morning."

Some parents find that rule setting is most effective when rules are stated in a more positive way.

"You may go out as far as the sidewalk."

"Cookies are for afternoon snack."

Two year olds learn these rules informally as they come up. In Heath and Colby's family, how-

ever, there also was a monthly family meeting to talk about rules that the children were finding hard to follow. Although Heath and Colby were pretty young to understand the meaning of a family meeting, they really looked forward to eating rolls in the family room and drinking milk from coffee cups. At the meeting their parents described holidays and other special events that would soon occur. Each member of the family was given a special job. At Thanksgiving, for example, Heath was the roll man, and Colby was the cranberry man. Rules were defined broadly in this family. They specified not only acceptable behavior but also special activities that the children were allowed to do. Heath and Colby took turns mixing the orange juice, getting the newspaper, operating the garage door opener, and other household jobs that they found interesting. Their parents had gone to considerable effort to regulate the family environment.

In order for rules to serve their purpose, they should be applied consistently. At the same time situations always are changing, children are growing, and parents are developing new insights. Yesterday's rule may not be as good as today's idea. We visited one home in which the mother assured us that there *never* were exceptions to rules like "No dessert unless you finish your meal" or "No playing with things in stores." This degree of consistency seems artificially rigid. It does not help children learn about compromise, which is the rule in many real world settings.

Distraction

Jennifer, who was 16 months old, was at a family party. With so many people around to pay attention to her, Jennifer's parents were fairly relaxed about letting her

wander around on her own. Suddenly they became conscious of the fact that they hadn't heard from her for a while. After some searching, they found her sitting in a corner having the time of her life. She had discovered a box of chocolate candy and was busy figuring out how many pieces could fit into her mouth at the same moment. Jennifer's mother lifted her off the floor and carried her into the bathroom.

"Look in the mirror. You've turned into a chocolate Jennifer. We better get some soap and water and turn you vanilla."

By the time Jennifer returned to the party, the box of chocolates had disappeared, and Jennifer thought no more about it.

Younger children can often be distracted by cheerfully removing them from the situation, as Jennifer was removed from the chocolates. Other times they can be given a substitute object to replace one that is taken from them. As children get older, however, they hold onto their ideas more tenaciously, and it is harder to distract them.

Terry was visiting with her grandparents and wanted to feed the dog a biscuit. After Puddle-Pooch, who was already on the fat side, had had six biscuits, Grandma decided it was time to use some distraction.

"Puddle Pooch isn't hungry any more. Now it's time for Terry's lunch. Let's go in the kitchen and make a peanut butter sandwich. Would you like to help Grandma?"

Terry went into the kitchen without protest and went to work spreading peanut butter onto a piece of bread. The door bell rang, and by the time Grandma had answered it the peanut butter sandwich had disappeared. "You ate up that whole sandwich," said a surprised Grandma. "Puddle Pooch eat it all up," Terry answered proudly.

Distracting a two year old often requires some fast talking and imagination. Ryan was going through a stage of refusing to drink his milk. He no longer accepted the technique of sneaking in a sip of milk after every bite of mashed potatoes, so his parents tried verbal distraction:

Dad: Oh, I know what's wrong with this milk. It needs a little ketchup in it. (He pretended to pour the ketchup in the milk.) There—now I'm sure it will taste good. Try it and see.

Ryan: (Grabbing the milk and taking a sip) It tastes terrible!

Dad: It does? (sounding incredulous) Oh, of course. I know what's missing. Just a sprinkle of meow mix. Now I'm *positive* it will taste good.

Ryan: (Grabbing the milk and trying it again). It tastes terrible, terrible!

The game continued in this fashion until the milk was gone. In this case the distraction worked because it appealed to the two year old's sense of autonomy. Even though his father was only pretending to doctor the milk, Ryan got the opportunity to prove him wrong.

Distraction is an excellent way to avoid conflict when the reason for a parental request is complicated and hard to explain. Two year old children have difficulty understanding why they should eat certain foods but not others, why they have to go to bed at a certain hour, or why they cannot take a friend's toy home with them. Using humor and imagination to distract a child in these situations puts off the conflict until a later day, when perhaps the child will be better able to understand an explanation.

Distraction has definite limitations though. Both parents and children have to be in the right

mood. For their part parents need to feel pretty relaxed in order to be funny or imaginative. And children need to have some flexibility in their position too. Distraction does not work with a really serious conflict, or when there is not enough time to play games.

No Contest

A final way of avoiding conflict is to develop a very loose schedule in which children participate in the routine of parents and parents participate in the routine of their children. When we arrived at Mary's house, she was standing at the door with a cold hot dog in her hand. "One for me and one for you," she said to a bedraggled rag doll as she held the piece of hotdog up to its embroidered mouth. Mary's mother explained casually that the hot dog was Mary's breakfast. Mary always decides what she wants for breakfast and helps in its preparation.

After breakfast Mary and her mother do the housework together. Because Mary's mother sets a slow pace, Mary is able to join in. Mary plays with toys some of the time, but much of her play consists of helping or imitating her mother. We watched

them clean a sliding glass door, Mary on one side and her mother on the other. At lunch time Mary set the table, which was another favorite activity. As she put the silverware around the table her mother capitalized on the teaching opportunity. "Good, you remembered to take out three forks — one for mommy, one for daddy, and one for Mary."

This way of avoiding conflict is more than a technique. It is a lifestyle. We were impressed by the tranquility and intimacy that this approach to child rearing seemed to engender. Obviously it is limited to families with a small number of young children. More importantly, it requires a very child centered world view in which parents can accept the leisurely pace and indifference toward clutter that comes naturally to children. We visited with parents who felt guilty because they did not enjoy spending all day associating with their children. Yet we do not feel that all parents need to be as child centered as Mary's mother. This approach works well for parents who feel comfortable with it, but it can backfire when parents try to force themselves into such a role. Even the most child centered parents feel constrained at times adapting their activity to fit into a two year old's world.

WAYS OF RESOLVING CONFLICT

Explanation The most common sense technique for resolving a conflict is to talk about it. Words are pretty powerful for the two year old and parents can often accomplish miracles by offering a serious explanation.

A well-meaning relative had given Kori her first box of lollipops. Although Kori's parents were certain that a well-balanced diet would keep Kori from developing a "sweet tooth", they turned out to be wrong. Kori loved the lollipops and wanted to eat them for dinner. Her father thought that this was a good opportunity to teach Kori about nutrition. He had no idea how much she would understand but he gave Kori a brief explanation about the importance of protein. Kori forgot about the lollipops and went into the bedroom to get Raggedy Ann.

"Want your dinner, Raggedy? What you want for dinner? No lollipops. No, no lollipops. You want yogurt? Yogurt has protein. Special K has protein."

The use of explanation is a good technique when it works, but it doesn't work all the time. Some two year olds aren't verbal enough to follow explanations. Other two year olds, who have no problem with verbalization, become skilled at either making everything negotiable or else using the "let's talk about it" technique as a manipulation.

Kori had gone to sleep past her bedtime and was in that state that parents always dread, where she was simply too tired to go to sleep. After bringing two snacks, and telling several bald-headed chicken stories, her father finally said, "Now it's really time to go to sleep—good night and no more calling." As soon as he left the room, Kori started crying bitterly. This time her mother went into the room. "O.K., Kori, stop crying," she stated firmly. "Let's talk about it." Kori countered, "Let's talk about it in the living room."

Explaining rules to children actually encourages them to respond verbally. The children try to match the reasons of their parents with reasons of their own. Although their arguments may be pretty crude, and far from logical, parents who genuinely believe in explaining things to children will find themselves compromising. Some of the time the children will have a point.

When a two year old refuses to accept an explanation, and a compromise solution is not possible,

parents are placed in a position where they must invoke a stronger form of authority. Broadly speaking they can try to induce children to go along with them by offering some kind of reward, or they can coerce the children by using some form of punishment.

Rewards The parents in our study used rewards extensively. In fact all of the techniques for avoiding conflict could be described as rewards. Children feel rewarded when they are included in future plans, when they are offered a pleasant distraction, when they are praised for following a rule, and when they are allowed to share a common activity with parents. Rewards also were used on a systematic basis to overcome outstanding problems, such as using the toilet, shopping in the grocery store, and taking medicine. However, when resolving the day to day conflicts that occur in every family, parents were not especially inclined to use rewards. The pattern was one in which rewards were used more as a last resort in resolving conflict than as a preliminary step.

One reason may be that it is not always easy to think of an appropriate reward on the spur of the moment. Although most two year olds respond favorably to candy, few parents want to carry around a bag of candy to use as rewards. Another reason may be that two year olds have difficulty understanding the conditionality of a reward. Lennie was told by his parents that if he was a good boy and let the doctor see his tongue, daddy would buy him a little car. Lennie was terrified in the doctor's office and had a full blown temper tantrum. After the visit the real battle began. "I want car." "No," said Daddy, "you cried in the doctor's office." "Car, want car," screamed Lennie, who felt that having seen the doctor, he deserved the reward.

The primary reason for not using more rewards seems to be that parents simply do not think in terms of rewards during a conflict situation. The child's behavior upsets them, and they think in terms of punishment. To offer a reward goes against the grain. It is only after a problem recurs frequently, or is of special concern, that parents think through a systematic approach that involves some kind of reward.

Punishment The kind of punishment that the parents turned to most often was criticism. Usually they were careful to criticize the action rather than the child, but at the same time they were comfortable saying things like, "I don't like that" or "I'm very mad at you." This kind of statement felt right to the parents. It was emotionally honest. It also was a kind of explanation in that it went beyond saying "Stop it" or "No". The parents were trying to explain how they felt. For the most part the children seemed to perceive this criticism as a mild punishment. The parents regained their good humor after getting angry feelings off their chest, and the children went back to their activities, not much worse for the experience.

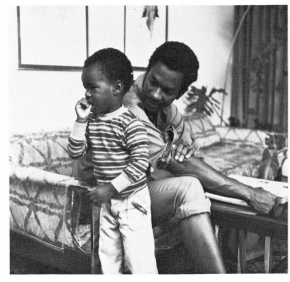

Another form of mild punishment was to deprive children of some privilege. Many parents were aware of the idea that the deprivation should be logically connected to the misbehavior. For example, if children wandered away from the yard, they were not allowed to play outside any more. Another common rule was that if siblings could not share, they had to play alone. This kind of deprivation was effective in many cases, but there were limitations. The logical consequence of not taking a nap is being overly tired, but few parents were willing to let their children get in such a state. A logical punishment for being destructive or excessively restless is to restrict the playing space of the child, but several parents found that this approach made their children even more destructive and restless. Parents also reported that denying children bedtime stories, favorite T.V. programs, or the chance to go outside, just because they had been "bad" did not have much impact on two year olds. The connection between the punishment and the crime was too vague.

For the worst offenses parents have stronger forms of punishment. The parents in our study considered spanking a strong form of punishment. Virtually all of them spanked their two year olds, but there were enormous differences in the amount of spanking parents did, the reasons for spanking, and their feelings about spanking. Some children were spanked as infrequently as once or twice a year, while others were spanked many times every day. Even the concept of what constitutes a spanking was different for different families. One parent tapped her child lightly on the rear after he ran out in the road, but still felt embarrassed at having used physical punishment. A second parent, who smacked her child on the legs twelve times during our visit, insisted that she seldom gave her child a spanking. When we questioned her further, we discovered that her definition of spanking was placing the child over her knee and hitting him with a brush.

Despite these differences the parents seemed to agree that spanking was reasonable in two situations. The first situation was one in which a child was doing something dangerous, such as playing with an electrical socket or riding a tricycle in the street. The other situation was when a child was exceptionally aggressive. Children who deliberately hit their parents in the face or bit their parents were very likely to be punished physically.

Even though parents used physical punishment, few of them defended it with much enthusiasm. They realized that spanking often occurred because they had lost control of their temper. They also realized that spanking worked because it intimidated the children, and most parents did not really want to foster a feeling of fear in their children.

In talking with the parents it seemed clear to us that there was a residue of guilt over spanking. As long as the parents felt they were not exceeding the "norm" for spanking, and as long as they could justify the spanking as being effective, this guilt did not surface. But when parents found themselves spanking more and more and being less and less effective, they began to feel frustrated and guilty. Terry liked to pull the leaves off houseplants. "I have smacked him and smacked him and smacked him," his mother told us, "but the more I spank him, the worse he gets."

A number of parents also told us that they had reconsidered their use of physical punishment when the children started to call their attention to it. When a two year old suddenly says, "Mommy, don't hit me," it may cause parents to see spanking in a new light.

The other form of strong punishment that parents used was isolation. This technique was the most popular way to handle temper outbursts. Children were told to go to their room (or bed) until they could behave more acceptably. In Brian's family his father had actually built a fort in the family room. When Brian was defiant, he was sent to his fort to play until all the bad feelings had gone away.

Typically children were allowed to decide when to come out. When they rejoined the family, they were hugged and reassured. Parents were amazed at the transformations in the children, from being defiant to being happy and wanting to please.

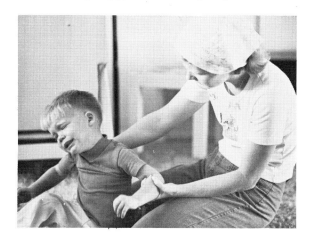

At dinner one night, Marty expressed his own tiredness by making the family miserable. He refused to eat his meat, kicked his sister, and finger painted on the table with his milk. His father issued a firm order. "Go into your room and don't come out until you can eat your dinner." Marty returned in good spirits a few minutes later. After dinner Marty was on his best behavior and even picked up his toys without being asked. Finally, it was getting late and his mother suggested that they go get ready for bed. Marty responded with genuine surprise, "I a good boy. I don't got to go in my room."

The isolation technique also worked well in Antonia's family. The only problem was that Antonia hated to go to sleep at night. She inevitably crept out of bed and as the family expressed it, "camped out in the hall." Using the bedroom as a form of isolation during the day contributed to a night time problem. The behavior of Marty and Antonia illustrate some of the side effects that isolation can produce. It is a very powerful form of punishment for two year olds because it elicits separation fears.

Although many professional psychologists recommend ignoring a temper tantrum, the parents in our study did not respond in this way. They reacted to a temper tantrum by sending the child away. Pretending not to hear a screaming fit was either too difficult or too unnatural. Instead the parents made it clear that they heard and that they disapproved. At the same time they gave the children a way to save face, or perhaps we should say a way to change their face. As soon as they felt better, the children were free to leave their exile and rejoin society.

Whining and grumpiness were not major concerns of the parents in our study. Apparently they are more characteristic of older children. Grumpiness might be handled with isolation too, especially if a family has established a habit of dealing with anti-social behavior in this way. However, it really is a different situation. The child has a greater degree of self control and is more capable of communicating than in the case of a temper tantrum. Some families find that a magical approach will work with grumpiness. Betty's family had bought a small, comfortable rocking chair and put it in the corner of the family room. It was called "the sweetening chair," and it was a magic chair. Whenever one of the children was acting cross or upset, she was asked to sit in the sweetening chair so that the chair could make her sweet again. No one ever sat in the chair except when she was feeling grouchy. One day Betty was sitting in the sweetening chair on her own. "What are you doing in the sweetening chair?," her mother asked. "Sh-sh don't talk me, Mommy, I turning sweet."

As we looked at the different techniques that parents used to avert or resolve a conflict situation, we found ourselves making value judgments. Although we recognize children's need for limits, we found families in which punishment was breaking down the attachment bond between parents and children. Any form of punishment can become so punitive that it threatens a child with loss of love. This happens when parents use punishment too often. Whether it is spanking, yelling, isolating, or depriving a child of privileges, a punishment loses its power if it is over used. The child stops responding to the parent because he feels he has little to lose. Both children and parents are caught in a vicious cycle. Parents step up the punishment because it is ineffective, and children withdraw their allegiance even more. When parents find themselves in this kind of situation, it is time to reduce the level of punishment and concentrate on avoiding conflicts or resolving them through rewards.

DAILY ROUTINES

The plan for this section is to take a close look at the major routines that punctuate a day in the life of a two year old. As we watch families carrying out their daily routines, we will have an opportunity to see the different ways in which families handle conflicts. Even more important we will see how families use conflict as an opportunity for learning and an impetus for growth.

Eating Some of the happiest moments within each family are associated with eating. Happy moments include shared cooking time, birthday parties, picnics, holiday dinners, or special treats like a bag lunch on the porch or dinner at a fast

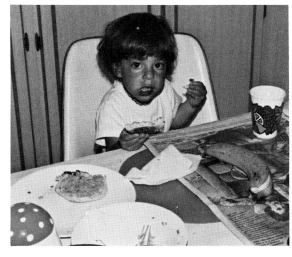

food restaurant. On the other hand, some of the most stressful moments in a family are associated with eating too. Although no two families are alike, we found a consistent pattern in the eating problems that were reported. Parents told us repeatedly that breakfast and lunch usually went fine, but that trouble occurred at dinner. Heather's mother related a typical story:

Heather: I want pasgetti and meatballs. I don't want chicken."

Mother: "Heather, I didn't make any spaghetti, and you love chicken. Why don't you try it."

Heather: "I want pasgetti and meatballs. I don't like chicken."

Mother: "Heather, you had spaghetti and meatballs for lunch. Here's your chicken. Do you want it or don't you?"

Heather: "I don't want chicken."

Mother: "I'll give you one last chance. Either you eat your chicken right this minute or I'll take your plate away."

Heather proceeded to play with the chicken and not eat it. She got one more chance and then the food was taken away. The episode ended with an enormous temper tantrum.

Meal Time Problems Two to three year old children are struggling to grow up and being grown up means making your own decisions. At breakfast and lunch many children are allowed to decide what they want to eat, at least they are given several choices. The children see that different members of the family eat different cereals or sandwiches. Naturally they assume the same kind of freedom is possible at dinner. Two year old children also become aware that there is food around which does not meet the eye. Heather certainly suspected, if she did not know, that there was another can of spaghetti and meatballs in the cupboard. Once children learn that a supply of their favorite food is hidden somewhere in the kitchen, they become upset with parents for depriving them at dinnertime.

We are not suggesting that two year olds are justified in demanding their favorite foods at dinner. It would be a lot more work to fix separate dinners for different family members, although we visited homes in which this was done. Our point is that conflicts arise at dinner because children are not given the same latitude they enjoy at other meals. The rules change at dinnertime and children need extra time to realize and accept this fact.

Dinner is different in other ways too. For most families it is the most formal meal of the day. The meal lasts longer and children are expected to stay at the table. Brian's father had just come back from a two day trip. His mother welcomed him home with a particularly nice dinner and had even made it a festive occasion by placing candles on the table. Brian sat politely at the table for the first half of the meal, but when his sister asked for more beans and his father told something to his mother that he couldn't understand, Brian had had enough, and slipped down from his youth chair. "Brian, please stay at the table," his mother requested. "We want tonight to be a very happy time for all of us." Brian, who saw no connection between happiness and sitting at the table, shouted "no" defiantly, and dashed around the room. "Brian," his mother cajoled, "I have a lovely dessert for you. As soon as you finish eating your meat, you can have dessert." "I don't want my meat, I want dessert." "Brian," his father insisted in a firm voice, "you heard what your mother said. Now let me put you back in your chair."

Staying in his chair is not much of an issue for Brian at breakfast and lunch. He usually watches Sesame Street while eating breakfast, and at lunch time he often eats on the run. Although he is not supposed to take food in the living room, he can eat a sandwich while playing in the family room or outside on the patio. Breakfast and lunch end when he is through eating. Brian is not required to sit and wait

for his sister or parents to finish. The atmosphere is casual and spontaneous. Sometimes the family eats together and other times everyone eats more or less independently.

A second way in which dinner time differs from other meals is in the attention that is paid to good manners. Many two year olds enjoy playing with their food. Chocolate pudding, they discover, makes fine fingerpaint, bread is good for making balls, and peas and lima beans are fun to squash. Although this kind of behavior is discouraged by parents, it is most likely to be tolerated at breakfast or lunch. At dinner time, since everyone is eating together, parents expect children to use a fork instead of their fingers, to take moderate bites instead of stuffing their mouths with food, and to ask politely for food instead of grabbing it. These niceties are welcomed at other meals too, but enforcement is lax.

A third difference between dinner and other meals is the amount of exclusive attention the child is given. Many fathers do not eat breakfast or lunch with their children, so the children are able to enjoy the undivided attention of their mothers during these meals.

Mother: "What would you like for lunch, Kori? Would you like a peanut butter sandwich or a cheese sandwich?"

Kori: "Cheese sandwich. Make a cheese sandwich."

Mother: "Let's open the refrigerator door. Cheese, where are you hiding? Are you underneath the pickle? No. Are you behind the horseradish?"

Kori: "I find the cheese. I make a sandwich."

Mother: "Will you make me a sandwich too? I'm hungry."

(Mother and Kori jointly get the sandwiches together and sit at the table.)

Mother: "Would you like to pour your own milk?"

(Kori begins to pour the milk into her glass.)

Kori: "Uh-Oh I spilled it!"

Mother: "Do you need a sponge?"

(Kori wipes up the milk, eats part of the sandwich, and then takes the cheese out of the second half.)

Kori: "I'm making a snowman."

Mother: "Yes, that does look like a snowman. I see his head and his tummy."

In contrast dinnertime conversation is more likely to revolve around adult-oriented topics, as the parents share their daily experience with each other. Parents also look forward to relaxing during the evening meal. The problem is that when parents are winding down, the two year old may be winding up. Eating a leisurely meal is relaxing for mother and dad, but a two year old may find it torture to sit at the table for more than five minutes. What begins as a quiet evening may end up with a shouting match, a temper tantrum, and an agreement by both parents that "something has to be done about that kid."

A good way for parents to identify possible solutions to the evening meals is to think about the difference between meals in their own family. How different are the expectations at dinnertime? Once parents have clarified their expectations, it is easier to evaluate new ideas that might improve dinnertime. The parents we visited suggested a number of ideas. The most radical solution is for children and parents to eat separately. In these families the children often eat before the father comes home and then go to bed soon afterward. This idea may eliminate dinnertime hassles, but it also can eliminate most of the daily interaction between children and their father. Usually families opt to stay together at dinnertime.

Jennifer's mother took advantage of her daughter's interest in helping in the kitchen by involving her in the preparation of the evening meal. "We have so much to do tonight," she commented to Jennifer. "We have to fix the salad, and shell the peas and warm up the rolls, and set the table. I'm lucky you are here to help me." As Jennifer and her mother shelled the peas, the conversation went on. "I hope everybody sits at the table tonight and finishes their dinner. You and I are working so hard to make this dinner nice." "I'm working hard making dinner," Jennifer agreed.

Chris' parents solved the dinner problem in a different way. They realized that the food smearing and tossing inevitably began when the children were

bored with the conversation. During the main part of the meal when they really wanted the children to remain quietly at the table, they directed the conversation to the children. If the children wanted to leave after finishing their dinner, they could. Dessert and coffee time was reserved for grown-up talk.

Other solutions that parents used with partial success included allowing the children to bring one toy to the table, relaxing about manners and giving the children an opportunity to play for a few minutes between the main course and dessert. Rosina's family had their greatest success when Rosina was allowed to be the waitress. Amazingly enough Rosina learned to carry the plates one at a time from the dinette to the kitchen counter.

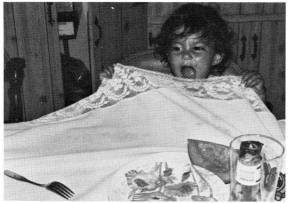

Eating Out Eating dinner at someone else's house can be particularly trying. "I love going to my mother's" declared one of the parents in our study, "but when she invites the family to dinner, I am a nervous wreck." As we questioned further, Susan's mother described the last family get together. The problem began as soon as Susan discovered that everyone but she had a steak knife. "I want that," said Susan, pointing a forefinger at her mother's knife. Susan was about to insist but was distracted by a plate of pickles. Delighted to have averted the first burst of tears, her mother gave her a pickle. "Be careful, take a tiny bite," her mother warned a little too late. Susan had taken an enormous bite and was gagging on it. From then on

things went from bad to worse. Susan spilt her milk, spit out her carrots, and broke a dessert dish. "Grandma remained calm and cheerful," Susan's mother reported, "but I was a nervous wreck."

Although a dinner out does not always include as many catastrophies as Susan's mother described, it is true that two year olds are not quite ready to join polite society. At one moment they are on their best behavior, basking in the glory of extra attention. At the next moment they are trying out some attention-seeking antic that parents interpret as obnoxious. Fortunately most hosts, especially if they happen to be grandparents, are delighted with having a two year old around and are quick to forgive and forget. Parents need to recognize that with time and practice even ornery two year olds will improve their eating out behavior and become "socially acceptable."

Parents also can alleviate some problems by taking precautions. Pete's mother solved the spilling problem by bringing along a plastic tablecloth and putting it under Pete's chair. Allison's mother had a kit of miniature toys that were used only when eating out.

Mandy's mother used this idea very successfully in restaurants. She put together a special kit to be used only in restaurants. It contained a small picture book, a tape measure, some seals, some water color markers, and paper. "I also take a cup of fruit in a little plastic container," Mandy's mother explained, "so she won't fill up on bread while we are waiting to be served. She is an absolute doll in the restaurant and we love to go out to eat." Although it is not necessary to have such an elaborate kit, the idea of taking materials for a quiet, table activity is excellent. Of course, the situation in a fast food restaurant is different. There is little waiting for food, and two year olds typically adore the informal atmosphere. They can get up from the table, talk as loudly as they want, and eat their favorite foods.

Snacks

Many of the families we visited were comfortable with the compromises they had worked out around meal times but were still having a problem with snacks. Families find themselves having to make all kinds of decisions

about snacking. How often should the child be allowed to snack? What should he be allowed to eat? Where should snacking be permitted? But before a family decides what kinds of rules to enforce about

the where's, what's and when's of snacking, they have to come to grips with the purpose that they would like snacking to serve.

The parents in our study gave snacks to children for two major purposes. First, they were allowed because the children seemed to be hungry.

Most two year olds have a relatively small capacity for food. they can feel perfectly full at the end of breakfast and then quite hungry two hours later. The second reason for giving snacks was quite different. Snacks were used as a reward to manage the behavior of children. Although families differed a great deal in their use of food as a reward, almost all families used it to some extent.

When snacks were used to tide children over between meals, nutritional foods were emphasized, and children were surprisingly receptive to them:

"My tummy needs a snack," Angela insisted as she pulled her mother into the kitchen.

"Well, I guess that it does," her mother responded. "Do you suppose your tummy would like celery with cottage cheese in it or a box of raisins?"

"I tuppose wants raisins," Angela decided. At this point Angela brought out a snack tray. "How about I eat my snack on the porch?"

"Fine idea," her mother agreed.

Even the child who refuses vegetables at meal time may be delighted with a snack that consists of a piece of fruit, a strip of raw carrot, or a slice of cucumber, uncooked squash, or cauliflower. Other nutritious snacks that families used included squares of cheese, frozen yogurt, sesame seeds, peanut butter on celery and frozen fruit juice in a dixie cup.

When using food as a reward, parents were much more likely to resort to sweets or junk food. Common examples include giving children a piece of gum for good behavior in the grocery store, giving them candy for learning to use the toilet, putting medicine in a sweetened drink, and handing them cookies to stop their crying. The practice of using dessert as a reward for eating the main course was virtually universal.

Using snacks in these two different ways sets up

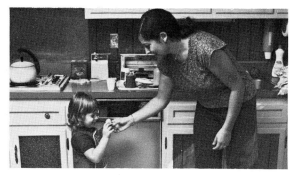

a confusing situation for children. Parents are sending the children contradictory messages. One message is that eating certain foods is important because they are nutritious. The other message is that eating sweets is important because they are a sign of good

behavior. On the one hand parents discourage sweets as not nutritious, but on the other hand they increase the significance of sweets by linking them to good behavior. This inconsistency comes about for a good reason. Parents sincerely want their children to eat nutritious foods, but at the same time they do not want to give up the very effective technique of offering sweets as a means of managing behavior.

We are not implying that parents should give up this technique. Just as the rules change for different meals, so can the rules about snacks change with different situations. But parents can recognize this inconsistency and anticipate a similar kind of ambivalence in their children. The children may accept the importance of eating nutritious food and still have a strong desire for sweets and junk food.

Some families in our study tried to be completely logical about snacks and desserts. They allowed no sweets in the house. However, it usually turned out that the children had discovered nutritious substitutes which were artificially sweetened, such as yogurt or cereal. Sugar is added to so many

food products that it seems impossible to avoid it altogether. We also found that when a certain sweet or junk food was completely prohibited, it turned into a "forbidden fruit" and was craved all the more. Parents who did not keep an excessive number of sweets around the house but who didn't get upset if their children ate sweets every once in a while seemed to have the most success.

From a two year old's point of view, snacks provide an important means of expressing autonomy. Like Angela, many children are given an opportunity to make a limited choice. They are permitted to feed themselves snack food and, within limits, to choose where to eat it. Angela enjoyed following her mother's rule about using a snack tray because she perceived it as an opportunity to be grown up, rather than a restriction of her autonomy.

Where families allow children to take part in making a snack, there are extra bonuses. The child not only develops fine motor skills by spreading, mixing, pouring, spooning, and opening and closing jars, he also learns to use language to describe his various activities. As he separates the sections of a tangerine, dips a butter spreader into a jar of peanut butter, or watches his frozen yogurt melt in the heat, he is learning about real world properties.

Dressing

Terry's mother greeted us at the door. "Just in time," she assured us. "I just got Terry dressed up and ready for his picture." At this moment Terry strolled into the room. On top he was wearing an attractive plaid shirt neatly buttoned up; on the bottom he was wearing nothing. "Oh, no, not again," his mother sounded off in dismay. "Ever since this kid learned to undress himself I can't get him to keep his clothes on."

Other parents in the study had similar complaints. Just as two year olds want to express their autonomy by choosing their own food, they want to choose what to wear, and often this choice is to wear as little as possible. The preferred state of dress for many two year olds is a T-shirt and underpants (or diapers).

At the same time clothes are an important part of a two year old's sense of identity. Shoes are particularly important. In the first place shoes go on feet and ever since the baby first discovered his toes at six months old, feet have held a special fascination. Furthermore, from the child's point of view, the ritual that goes on in a shoe store makes the buying of shoes an awesome occasion. He sits down in a special chair all by himself, a man comes over with a big silver shining thing, and puts his foot inside it. The silver thing closes itself around his foot. Then a man comes with an armful of boxes. He keeps taking shoes out of the box and fitting them on until he finds exactly the right shoe. Then, with even greater solemnity, the shoes get wrapped up and paid for. The child may even be given a balloon to mark the event. It is no wonder then that children assign special significance to shoes.

Some children get attached to one pair of shoes and refuse to wear anything else. It is almost as if the shoes are a part of them, and if they changed to different ones, it would change them in some sort of disastrous way. Kori became attached to a pair of red sneakers, and insisted on wearing her red sneakers with a long pink party dress to Thanksgiving dinner. Other children are more like Jon, who decided that his sandals were for playing at the park, his sneakers

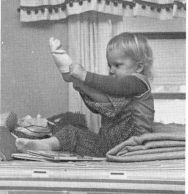
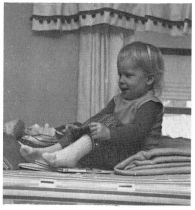

were for nursery school, and his brown shoes were for McDonald's. Some children won't wear shoes at all but insist on carrying the shoes with them.

Most of the parents in our study allowed their children some sort of choice in the selection of clothes. Inevitably there were problems. From a parent's viewpoint the children seemed excessively rigid. Why must it be the same dress every Sunday, thought Jenny's mother. Jenny was especially attached to a dress that had bells sewn into the hem, which she called her ring-ding dress. From a child's viewpoint, however, it may seem that parents are awfully rigid in their ideas too. Parents seem to have the peculiar notion that certain clothes do not go with each other, like red sneakers with a pink party dress.

Even if parents are not concerned about their child being stylish, limits have to be set on the free choice of clothing. There are times when children insist upon wearing something that either is or ought to be in the washing machine. There are also hot days when children decide to wear a turtleneck sweater and cold days when they would like to wear shorts. Sometimes an inappropriate choice can become an opportunity for learning how to compromise.

Jason's grandmother bought him a pair of swimming trunks with a sailboat applique. Not surprisingly Jason wanted to wear his boat pants the next morning even though it was snowing out.

"You can't go out with boat pants," his mother explained. "Boat pants are for summer when it's hot."

"I hot," Jason argued. "I want to wear boat pants."

"I'll tell you what," his mother suggested. "We will put your boat pants on now and **pretend** it's summer. Then before you go **out, we will** put on long pants."

Like the Jason pant problem, many of the problems around dressing can be solved if there is plenty of time. The day stretches on forever when you are two years old, and it's hard to understand why parents are so rushed.

Jennifer had learned to put on her own shoes, and was generally outraged if anyone offered to help her. One day the family was taking off on a vacation and everyone was in a grand hurry. "Please Jennifer, put your shoes on," her mother begged. "We have to leave for the airport right away." Jennifer tried to hurry but it was hurrying that made her awkward. "You put my shoes on, Mommy," Jennifer finally said in tears, "I'm too little."

Some two year old children, like Jennifer, identify dressing skills with being grown up. Being able to put on your shoes, or button your shirt, is an important way to express autonomy. These children spend long hours practicing dressing skills. We watched Keisha struggle patiently for 15 minutes to buckle a pair of sandals. When she stood up they were on the wrong feet. No matter, she sat down again and spent another 15 minutes switching them around.

Two year olds who are intent on practicing dressing skills may get in the habit of changing their clothes several times a day. This habit can be distressing to parents because the clothes that are removed are left on the floor and get dirty. In Nicole's family this situation had taken an unexpected, and amusing, turn. Nicole had been reminded so often that her clothes became dirty when they touched the floor that she started changing her underpants after every trip to the bathroom. After all, she explained, the panties touched the floor when she sat on the toilet, so they were dirty.

Some two year olds show little interest in learning to dress themselves. This is especially true of first born children who have no older brothers or sisters to emulate. In these families the parents often have established a pattern in which dressing is a leisurely social occasion. It has been a time when the parents and children converse, play silly games, and sing songs. Parents should recognize that children with this kind of experience are going to learn to dress themselves later than other children. This is perfectly all right as long as parents have the time and energy to help them. However, if the parents feel the children need to learn dressing skills right away, a special effort will be needed to overcome the pattern of the past. The children are likely to resist dressing themselves because they enjoy both the social stimulation and the feeling of being waited upon. Their way of expressing autonomy is to insist that this pattern be continued.

The most effective way to meet this problem is to show children that learning how to dress can be part of a social occasion too. Pete's mother, for example, suggested that they take turns. "My turn with your socks," she said cheerfully as she put the socks on. "Now it's your turn to pull them up." She

always engineered the sharing so that Pete finished the task. Kelly's mother used singing. As Kelly stuck her arms through the sleeves in her shirt, her mother sang, "This is the way Kelly puts on her shirt, puts on her shirt, puts on her shirt." Gradually Kelly assumed more and more responsibility for putting on her clothes, and her mother's job was just to sing.

Washing Up When we arrived at Danielle's house, she was just finishing a breakfast of French toast and syrup. "I wash my hands all by myself," she told her father as he helped her down from the high chair. "Cold water first," she told herself as she turned on the right hand faucet. After a good five minutes of hand scrubbing, Danielle's father suggested that her hands were clean and handed her a towel. Like most two year olds Danielle enjoyed washing her hands because she could play in the water.

Brushing teeth is also a favorite activity for most two year olds. It's a new accomplishment that allows them to play with water and makes them feel grown up. Squeezing the toothpaste is a great deal of fun, and if parents do not do some careful supervising, a large portion of the tube gets used in a single brushing.

Unless parents mention the nasty term, "hair wash," bath time too is great fun for the two year olds. The earlier fear of going down the drain has probably been conquered by now, and the child enjoys the opportunity of splashing, pouring, making waves, and mixing the water with soap. A favorite activity is lining up toys on the side of the tub and making them dive in.

Hair washing is quite a different story. Most two year olds at some time or other have gotten soap in their eyes, and are very resistant to hair washing. Families either have to put up with some crying and screaming or find a way to get around it.

Laurie was basically a mild and pliable child who followed her parents' suggestions in the most agreeable way. But somehow or other the sight of a shampoo bottle sent her into a frenzy. Hair wash night was dreaded as much by her parents as it was by her, but finally her mother got an idea. She took Laurie to the beauty parlor and let her watch several ladies getting their hair washed. That night Laurie and her mother played beauty parlor. They sat Laurie's doll on the edge of the bathtub, and Laurie became the shampoo lady. "Stay still and keep your head back, Doll," her mother commented. "Don't cry, Doll," her mother went on, "Laurie won't let the soap get in your eyes." After a while Laurie agreed to put a tiny tiny bit of shampoo into her own hair, and her mother became the shampoo lady.

Less elaborate solutions to the hair washing problem include the use of a water pik, a hand spray, or "desensitization" washes in which the parent concentrates on being gentle rather than getting the hair clean. Another possibility is to let children play with a bubble pipe. While the child looks up to watch the bubbles fly, the parent can rinse away the shampoo without getting soap or water on the child's face.

Housework

Kelly's grandmother had invited the family to brunch. "Do you suppose you could be finished with the housework in an hour and get over early?" Grandma asked. "I think so," Kelly's mother asserted, "as long as Kelly doesn't decide she would like to help me."

Most two year olds really enjoy helping with the housework. The favorite things to help with, of course, are usually those things where the parent least wants help. Children love to wash dishes, water plants, or disperse the cleaning sprays. Some of the families that we visited were quite successful at capitalizing on their two year old's desire to help out. Jon's mother took the extra time to teach Jon how to water plants without drowning them, and how to wash dishes without simultaneously washing the floor. She found that Jon was a genuine help with the housework, and was even able to push the vacuum cleaner around.

The major issue concerning housework was picking up. Parents differed greatly in their expectations. Some parents expected children to be responsible for picking up their own toys from the age of 18 months; others thought that four years old was about the right age. Most of the families felt that two year olds should participate to some extent in picking up.

Looking more closely at the conflict over picking up, it appeared that the real issue was the use of

toys in certain parts of the house. Toys scattered in a child's bedroom were not too upsetting. It was the mess in the family room, or the clutter in the kitchen, that caused most of the trouble. Of course children transport their toys to the "living" rooms of the house as soon as they begin to walk (or even crawl). But it seems that between the ages of two and three many parents hope this situation will change.

One reason for expecting change is that the children are more able to play independently, which suggests that they might play independently in a bedroom. Another reason is that the children are more able to understand explanations, which leads parents to think that they should be able to understand why picking up is necessary. A third reason is that the patience of parents simply gives out. They get tired of the clutter and figure they have put up with it long enough.

In the strictest households we visited parents tried to enforce the rule that children get out only one thing at a time. When they were through with that toy, it was to be put back before getting out another. Some parents commented that their children were trained to play with one thing at a time at nursery school, so why not do the same at home. This rule was more a vision in the minds of parents than a reality. We visited only one home in which the child really practiced what the parent preached, and this home was run very much like a school. In other cases the rule led to continual conflict. Apparently the children saw their homes as being different from a school environment, and they were unwilling to accept the same rules.

Most families aimed for one or two general cleanups a day. This practice was successful if parents helped. If they tried to force a child to pick up on his own, a slowdown, or even a sitdown, was likely. This suggests to us that two year old children

do not really accept the need for picking up, but if it is part of a pleasant social experience, they are happy to participate.

When parents help pick up, it also makes the activity like an adult job. Participating in an adult activity is much more likely to appeal to a two year old's sense of autonomy. Several families had provided toy boxes or baskets in the living room. In this way toys could be picked up without taking them to the bedroom. This idea makes picking up more convenient, and it also may make it more important in the eyes of a child. From a child's viewpoint taking toys to the bedroom may seem almost insulting. These toys are his most precious possessions, and they are being excluded from the important parts of the house. After all, bedrooms are used to keep children in their place. Children are sent there to finish temper tantrums and to sleep alone at night. Making them keep their toys in the bedroom may seem like one more example.

A toybox or a basket also encourages picking up because it is fun to throw things in. In the long run, however, it discourages order because it is hard to find anything without emptying the whole box. The most easily understood reason for picking up is that it keeps toys from getting lost or misplaced. Two year olds readily understand this principle with individual toys. They enjoy finding the pieces and fitting them together. But when the toys are then piled in a toybox, the purpose for picking up becomes obscure.

An alternative that seems especially good for two year olds is a shallow cabinet, i.e. a set of narrow shelves with a door. Opening and closing the door makes the cabinet an exciting container, while the shelves allow the child to find individual toys easily. For parents who are very intent on teaching a two year old to pick up, we would recommend building such a cabinet for the family room, kitchen, or wherever the child plays most often.

Regardless of how ingenious or persistent parents are, most two year olds will continue to see picking up as a social activity. They will not be very interested in doing the job by themselves. Parents may think that only a few weeks, or months, of picking up with the children will be sufficient to model this behavior. Our study indicates, however, that it takes a much longer time for children to internalize the value of a tidy room. It is reasonable to introduce the idea of picking up at this age, but it is unrealistic to expect the lesson to be learned fully. It also is a good idea to store away the toys that a child is no longer interested in so that there is at least some limit to the amount of mess a child can create.

Toilet Training

Toilet training was a continuing concern of the parents in our study. The following kinds of comments were made over and over again.

> "He was practically trained at eighteen months and now he won't even sit on his potty."

> "When she has to make a BM, she goes over to the corner and makes it there."

> "She always tells me she has to go right after she wets her pants."

> "She insists on standing up to 'pee' and wets all over the floor."

Becoming toilet trained is a major accomplishment for young children, and if it is not accomplished by the age of three, it can become a major source of conflict between children and parents. Different factors come into play in influencing the ease with which children are toilet trained. Children must be ready both physiologically and psychologically. They must have the neuro-muscular coordination to control their bowel and bladder functions, and they must be able to recognize an advantage in using the toilet rather than diapers.

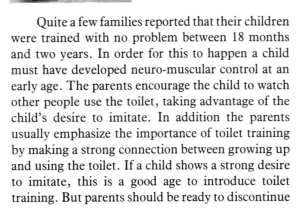

Quite a few families reported that their children were trained with no problem between 18 months and two years. In order for this to happen a child must have developed neuro-muscular control at an early age. The parents encourage the child to watch other people use the toilet, taking advantage of the child's desire to imitate. In addition the parents usually emphasize the importance of toilet training by making a strong connection between growing up and using the toilet. If a child shows a strong desire to imitate, this is a good age to introduce toilet training. But parents should be ready to discontinue this training if it becomes clear that the child is not physically ready.

By the age of two many children are physically ready for toilet training, but they have developed strong ideas about doing things their own way. Once a child's sense of autonomy comes into conflict with toilet training, the process will be more difficult and may be prolonged. This kind of conflict is a common occurrence, and parents should not be overly concerned. It simply means that toilet training will be a bit harder. Some of the families in our study who found themselves in this position put off further toilet training until their children were 2½ or even 3, when the children would be more likely to accept toilet training as a sign of being grown up.

Depending on the needs and desires of the family, as well as the inclination of the family, toilet training can be accomplished with the two year old by a quick method that involves a major investment of time over a short period, or a slow method that requires a less concentrated effort over a longer period of time. The short methods are usually based on some sort of behavior modification technique where the child is rewarded consistently when he uses the toilet.

Sometimes children are promised a reward that will make them feel grown up, such as a pair of pretty panties like older girls wear, or a big bed instead of a crib. However, the most effective reward system consists of giving children a special treat, such as candy, every time they use the toilet. One of the most popular fast methods advocates giving children a sweet drink. That way the children get rewarded and also have to go to the bathroom again soon. The logic of the technique is that by rewarding children many times over a short period, the habit will be established and the tangible rewards can be withdrawn.

The slower methods of toilet training depend on modeling, persuasion, or an appeal to the child's desire to be grown up. This process can take a long time. We found a number of two year olds who had developed arguments against using the toilet. Shawn's was the most elaborate. He was not a baby, but neither was he a big boy. He was a little boy and would remain so until he was three years old, when he would start using the toilet.

To some extent two year olds who present this kind of argument may be afraid of failing, and so they resist trying to use the toilet. Perhaps they find the toilet uncomfortable or frightening. Quite often they simply enjoy going to the bathroom in their diapers. Going to the bathroom is a habit, and they have developed the habit of eliminating intentionally in their diapers.

The times when toilet training becomes a real hassle is when parents become punitive. Parents who spanked their children because they had accidents told us that their children got worse. Where parents were relaxed in their attitude and understanding about accidents, they were not apt to have much difficulty. Ursula's parents took a laissez faire approach to toilet training, and were delighted with Ursula's own interest in keeping herself dry. One day, however, after several days without an accident, her father found her in front of the bathroom standing in a puddle of water. "Daddy, look what happened — wee wee came too early!"

If a nursery school is willing to accept a child who is not yet toilet trained, training may be accomplished quickly in the nursery school setting. The child sees other children using the toilet and doesn't want to be different. However, a child who continues to have problems with training will get teased by the peer group. Parents should be alert to this. The child who is shamed by a toileting accident may develop other bad feelings about himself.

In general, since the advent of disposable diapers, toilet training is less of an issue than it used to be. Parents need to remember that in good time all children are toilet trained and the more relaxed they can be about it, the easier it will happen.

Sleep Time

Between the ages of one and three the amount of sleep a child requires decreases gradually. Naptime becomes a time for arguments between parent and child. Many parents feel that naptime is as important for them as it is for their child. They need the time to relax and be by themselves. Parents who were not ready to give up their own rest time found different solutions. Sean's mother solved her problem by calling naptime "the quiet hour." Sean is expected to go to his room and rest in bed. He may have books and small toys in bed with him or he may nap. Michael's mother found that Michael was willing to take a nap if he was allowed to sleep in his parents' bed. Theresa's mother used a pretend solution to help Theresa nap. "I know that you're not tired but the dolls are, so please rest with the dolls."

While some families struggle to enforce a nap with their children, other families are working out ways to prevent their child from napping. Their complaint is either that the children wake up cranky and are difficult to handle for the rest of the day, or that it's hard to get them to sleep at night. Sometimes families manage the transition period when the child is in the process of giving up the nap by arranging an afternoon outing. Others decide that it's just another one of those things that the family has to live through.

Bedtime problems topped the list of parent concerns in the 2-3 year old period. For some families the problem was getting the child to bed in the first place. For some it was ending the endless rituals of one more kiss, one more story, and one more glass of water. For others the problem was middle of the night prowling which often ended with everyone sharing the same bed.

Going to sleep is probably the most habit forming routine of all. Each person has a certain way of preparing for bed, of lying down, and of trying to relax and fall asleep. Deviations from this routine make sleep difficult. Most of the two year olds in our study had developed a bedtime routine. They brushed their teeth, drank water, and listened to stories in order to prepare for bed. They assumed their favorite sleeping position and tried to relax by sucking their thumb, clutching a blanket, being rocked, etc. For many of the children though, these procedures were not sufficient. They were unable to sleep and conflict developed with their parents.

Three different reasons for bedtime problems can be identified. Some children get so involved in the activities of the day that they cannot wind down and relax. A second reason may be a strong desire to keep playing. The child wants to hold onto the pleasures of the day just a little longer. Finally, children may be afraid of going to sleep because it involves separation from their parents. These reasons are not mutually exclusive. A child may resist going to bed for all three reasons.

In visiting with families we found that there was a natural response to these sleep difficulties. Families elaborated the routine of going to bed until a child felt more comfortable about going to sleep. This elaborated bedtime ritual became the unique creation of each family. It was not pre-planned but grew spontaneously as parents tried out different ideas.

Some bedtime rituals were designed primarily to help a child relax. The most common was singing a favorite song every night. Chris' father was able to relax Chris by giving him "one pat". Other rituals were designed to help a child accept the end of the day. They were the last exciting event. Andy would hide in his parents' bedroom and they would find him; then they would hide in his bedroom and he would find them. After that he went to bed. Robert's parents held him up to the window so that he could say goodnight to all the children in the neighborhood. Then he was put in his crib, whereupon he threw out all the stuffed animals except the monkey. During the last part of the ritual he sat in the crib and looked at a book, until it too was thrown out and he was ready to sleep. Some rituals were designed to minimize separation fears. Jodi's mother would hug her, pull away, and then come back for another hug and kiss. After three or four of these return hugs, she would leave the room. At Helaine's house the bedtime ritual consisted of her father standing in the hall where Helaine could see him. He stood there until she went to sleep.

Some parents don't believe in starting night time rituals. Jessica's mother was proud of the fact that at seven o'clock Jessica climbed into her crib and went to sleep without a fuss. Unfortunately, Jessica had a bout with an earache and had difficulty falling asleep. With no bedtime rituals to fall back on, bed time turned into a nightmare for the whole family. When Jessica's mother asked the pediatrician for sleeping pills, he suggested that the family try a bedtime story or a night light. Within a few days Jessica was going to sleep without problems and the family became an advocate of night time rituals.

Waking up in the middle of the night can be as big a problem as getting a child to sleep in the first place. Apparently two year olds have acquired the ability to dream. Sometimes they cry out in their sleep without waking up, and parents can only guess they were dreaming. At other times they wake up frightened but cannot say what they are frightened about. A few of our two year olds reported segments of a dream. John told his mommy a scary monster came and chased his daddy. Allison talked about the witch who was going to hit her with a corn thing. Once a child is wakened by a bad dream, getting him back to sleep can be difficult. The most common solution is either staying in the room until the child falls asleep or telling the child to come into the parents' bed. Some parents worked out magic solutions. Mandy's father always put a special magic kiss on her forehead to chase away the bad dreams. Allison's father opened the window and threw the dream witch out.

Several families in our study reported that they never had problems with sleep time. When we questioned these families further, it seemed that either the two year old slept in their room or in a room with older children. In some families the two year olds go to sleep in their own room but wander into the parents' room later and sleep there the rest of the night. Sleeping in the same room with another person eliminates many sleep problems.

A few of the children in our study had severe sleeping problems. They could not go to sleep for hours after going to bed, or awoke screaming in terror on a regular basis. Although it is not always clear what causes this kind of problem, it probably indicates that the child has a very strong fear of being left alone. This fear is latent in all children and may come to the surface after just a single frightening incident. It takes time to overcome.

The usual response is to physically hold the child until he falls asleep, or to lie down with the child. This is an effective and humane technique, but parents should be prepared to keep it up. Children get used to falling asleep in the arms of a parent, or while holding the parent's hand, and they have trouble sleeping without these comforts. If possible it probably is better to reassure the child simply by staying in the room.

We also would recommend that parents in this situation work on developing a bedtime ritual. Reading a story or turning on a night light may not be sufficient, and it will be necessary to experiment with different ideas, trying to find an activity that engages the interest of the child and relaxes him. By watching the responses of the child and listening to his suggestions, the parents will discover a routine that is special.

Some pediatricians advocate allowing children to cry themselves to sleep. This may be the only recourse in certain situations, but we would be concerned about repercussions.

Summary

We have mentioned some alternative solutions to problems involved in eating, dressing, sleeping, etc., but many other possibilities exist. A good way for parents to generate new ideas is to think about how conflict can be avoided. Can the rules be made more consistent? Is there a better way to plan ahead and to make clear to the child what to expect? Is there a way to distract the child, to defuse the problem by using humor and imagination? Can the child participate in a substitute activity? The size of a family affects the tactics that are chosen. A larger family must be better organized, which means that planning ahead, setting rules, and giving clear explanations is especially valuable. A small family, on the other hand, has more opportunity to handle routines through distraction, imaginative rituals, and compromise.

In discussing daily routines we have glossed over the non-routine events that happen nearly every day. These unusual events often are less private. Either the family goes out in public or other people come into the home. Because the experiences are out of the ordinary, the children become extra excited. This higher level of excitement, combined with the public character of unusual events, makes conflict more likely to occur and more difficult to resolve.

Parents do not have the same range of options. They have less time to explain, they are too busy or embarrassed to play games, and it is harder to compromise. Often they cannot deprive the children, apply logical consequences or use isolation. For their part the children are more wound up and less willing to listen to parental guidance. This dilemma is an occupational hazard for parents of two year olds to be accepted with as much grace as possible. Parents should not avoid public outings as a result, but neither should they over react when children misbehave. We observed the following incident while writing this book. It is typical of the kind of over reaction that can be seen every day in restaurants, grocery stores, and other public places.

A two year old was sitting in an ice cream parlor with his older sister and parents. The two year old put his hand on the table and began to finger his mother's spoon. She slapped his hand without looking down and continued talking with her husband. Several minutes later the boy fingered her spoon again. This time the mother picked up the spoon, and hit him across the fingers. Just at that moment the waitress arrived with a tray full of ice cream sundaes. The mother stuck a spoon in the boy's ice cream and told him to go ahead and eat. The child stared at the spoon with frightened eyes and never touched the ice cream.

Although we disapprove of the way this mother treated her son, exercising authority is an inevitable part of handling routines. Parents want their children to be obedient. Two year old children, on the other hand, seek to expand their sense of autonomy. This difference should not be exaggerated. Parents want their children to be autonomous, and children want to obey their parents. But there is a difference in perspective, and this difference leads to conflict. Conflict may lead to compromise, to greater communication between parents and children, to personal development on the part of both parents and children. Eventually conflict may be minimized, but it will not disappear. It is rooted in the different roles of parents and children.

If conflict is an inevitable part of routines, so is the joy of living together. As we watched the families in our study handle the problems and enjoy the benefits of everyday living with a two year old, we recognized that there is no one best child rearing style. Each family must discover the techniques that work best for them, and that are compatible with their philosophy and living style. At the same time each family must come to recognize that every child is different and that techniques that work well with one child may not be right for the next. In order to be effective, parents must be sensitive to the unique characteristics of each child.

Chapter II—Making Friends
Playing with Siblings 27
    Adjusting to a new baby 27
    Keeping up with older siblings 29
    Ways of responding to siblings 31
    Twins a special case 33
Playing With Friends 34
    Having an older friend 34
    Playing with another two year old 36
Styles of Playing 38
Group Experience 41
    Choosing the right setting 41
    A case study 42

Chapter II
Making Friends

The ability to make and keep friends is a valuable asset throughout a child's lifetime. Although we may not think of it in this way, it is a learned skill like reading, writing or riding a bicycle. Because friendship is so closely linked with happiness, it is a skill that we need to pay attention to as we monitor the development of the very young child.

In many traditional books on child development the social play of the two year old is described as "parallel." In parallel play children play along side of each other, aware of each other's presence but not really interacting. This may be an apt description of the play behavior of some two year olds, but it does not tell the whole story. Many children even younger than two years old have already learned to enjoy peer interaction and can play cooperatively for short bits of time. Certainly by two years old we can see the emergence of social skills if a child is given opportunities to play with other children.

In this chapter we will look at three aspects of playing with other children; playing with siblings, playing with friends, and playing in a group.

PLAYING WITH SIBLINGS

We were observing children in the waiting room of a pediatric clinic when one of the mothers started talking. "I always know the difference," this mother commented, "between the first babies and the ones with sisters and brothers." We asked her to explain. "Watch for yourself," she went on. "A first baby in a crowd of kids keeps his eyes glued on his mother and he won't move out of her sight. A second or third child in the same situation is right in the middle of the action looking over every kid in the place."

Although this mother's system of spotting firstborn children is by no means foolproof, it does point up a difference that many parents have noticed. The firstborn child, particularly if he lives a sheltered life, does not develop the same coping skills as a second or later born child. Faced with a threatening social situation, his best defense is to cling for dear life to a familiar hand or pant leg.

While the firstborn child may not be able to hold his own socially with other children, he has no problem managing his own parents. Many of the parents confess that their two year olds have already learned how to get what they want from each parent.

Adjusting to a New Baby Parents who have developed a close relationship with their first child are usually quite concerned when a new baby is born. They are prepared for all the symptoms of sibling rivalry—anger, jealousy, pouting, purposeful naughtiness, demanding behavior, and regression. Amy's mother, herself a firstborn who had been tormented by a younger brother, was particularly sensitive to the problems of sibling rivalry. About a month before her due date, she told Amy about the new baby that was growing in her uterus. She took Amy to visit a friend who had just had a new baby. She let Amy select crib sheets, pampers, and a toy for the new baby, and invited her to help set up the baby's room. She explained over and over to Amy that when the baby was ready to be born, she and Daddy would go to the hospital and Nana would stay at the house.

Before Amy's mother went to the hospital she instructed Nana to do two things. First, Nana was to take the tape recorder and a gift out of the closet. This is what the tape said, "Hello, Amy, I was just born and I am too little to talk — so Mommy is talking for me. I am happy that you are my sister. This is a present from me. Please open." As you might have guessed, the present was a baby doll.

The second thing that Nana was instructed to do was to bake a cake. Amy's mother had promised that they would have a birthday party when the baby came home from the hospital. Amy chose her favorite kind of frosting and helped Nana spread it on the cake, helping herself to generous portions in the process. When mother arrived home, the party took place. Amy had a good time blowing out the candle and eating the cake that the baby was too young to enjoy.

Although most parents don't go to quite these ends to avoid sibling rivalry, we did not find many of our two year olds upset about a new baby. As a matter of fact in many homes we got just the reverse. The two year olds were delighted with the new baby, and enjoyed sharing in the work. They sorted laundry and brought in diapers (many of the two year olds who were just mastering the toilet were pleased when the baby messed). They alternated between helping mother or dad take care of the baby and looking after their own doll and stuffed animals. Dolls that might have spent months in the bottom of the toy chest were resurrected and pressed into service.

This honeymoon period often doesn't last for long. After a while the two year old recognizes that the baby is getting a new kind of attention. Adults are not just taking care of her, they are laughing with her, cooing at her, and showing her off to friends. Just when the parents have relaxed their fear of sibling rivalry, the dreaded symptons appear. Alesha's mother's account is fairly typical. "At first when the baby was born everything was peaches and cream, but just recently now I'm seeing signs of jealousy. As soon as I begin to breast feed the baby, Alesha starts with "I got to go potty, hurry up!" In contrast to Alesha, Chad is forthright about his feelings toward his brother. "I don't like my brother," he informed his parents "because you are always holding him." When Chad's mother sang to the baby, "You are so beautiful," Chad voiced his protest. "Sing that song to me. Don't sing that to my brother."

In some cases the two year old has taken matters into his own hands and launched a direct attack on the younger rival. Stuart accidentally on purpose ran his bicycle into his baby sister. Lynn helped her little brother play with the Jack in the Box by taking over the toy. Nicole assumed an authoritarian role with her baby sister, wagging her finger and saying, "No, No!" whenever her sister put her thumb in her mouth or her hands in the apple sauce dish.

One reason parents give special attention to babies is because babies give that special attention back. Nothing quite equals the smile and gurgle of a young baby. Two year olds can be captivated by this responsiveness too, and in fact they have a natural ability to entertain babies. Parents can encourage them to use their range of two year old antics to amuse the baby. They also can show their two year old safe ways to handle the baby. Mary's mother taught Mary to play with the baby's feet instead of investigating his face. Brian's mother showed Brian how he could hold his baby sister's hand while she was drinking her bottle.

Sometimes the special attention that a baby receives can be modified or toned down. Brian's parents discovered that Brian was jealous of the way they took care of the baby at night. Sleeping in the same room, the baby woke him up when she cried out, yet he did not get the same degree of attention. This source of jealousy was removed by simply moving the baby to another room. Then Brian slept through the night and was no longer aware of the special care the baby received during the night.

In several families the parents made an extra effort to emphasize the "grownup" abilities of their two year old. Mary's mother reminded Mary that she could move around, run and jump, while the baby just had to lie on his back. Mary could drink from a cup and could even choose what to eat, while the baby always had to eat the same thing. The most dramatic way to demonstrate this idea is to take the two year old on a special outing—without the baby. One of Stuart's favorite activities was to go to Sambo's for breakfast with just his mother.

Keeping Up With Older Siblings

The two year old with an older sibling to contend with is in a different situation from the two year old with a new baby. Parents are often not as sensitive to feelings of jealousy in this situation. They are used to talking about how much the baby loves the older children in the family, and they may not notice when the love is tinged with rivalry. This is particularly true because early signs of rivalry are often hard to distinguish from imitative behavior.

Willie, who was just barely two, was watching his older sister Susan chewing gum. Willie didn't really know what gum was and was quite happy with the wrapper Susan gave him. He popped the wrapper in his mouth and started chewing. Apparently it didn't taste very good, and the family giggled at his expression of surprise and disgust.

Willie's demands for everything his sister got continued and after a while it stopped being funny. When Susie got penicillin for an ear ache, Willie wanted his penicillin too. When Susan put on a yellow dress for Sunday School, Willie cried bitterly until his mother let him wear a dress.

Emerging signs of sibling rivalry are not limited to this kind of "me too" behavior. A common way of expressing rivalry is learning to become a tease. According to his mother, Christopher, the youngest of three children, was a past master of this strategy. While we were visiting, he knocked down his sister's block building in a quick commando raid. Next he ran into his brother's room and came out with his favorite stuffed dog and hid it. This stuffed dog was the one possession his brother would **never** share.

Signs of sibling rivalry are becoming more and more obvious between two and three years old. Battles over possessions, privileges, and status in the family are continually rocking the household. From the point of view of parents, the most ridiculous things can create the biggest ruckus. Who gets to bring daddy the newspaper? Who is going to sit in the brown chair in front of the television set? Who gets the rose on the icing of the birthday cake? Who turns the pages in the "Goodnight Moon" story book?

Sometimes children attempt to protect their "turf" by demanding more attention from their parents. When Jodi's sister showed her mother her kindergarten papers, Jodi tugged at her mother's skirt saying, "I have something to tell you." Nicole's strategy was to appeal to her mother's sympathies. "Little Nicole is very sad because you won't pick me up. Little Nicole is a baby." Bernie's strategy was quite different. If he couldn't get his fair share of attention by being good, he would certainly get it by being bad. As soon as his father began playing with his brother, he deliberately sought out every naughty thing he could think of. His repertoire of bad things included walking across the back of the sofa, pulling on the curtain cord, pulling the books off the shelf and sticking both hands in the goldfish bowl. Despite themselves, Bernie's parents had to laugh at this sequence because it had become a ritual. The two year old's need to be repetitive shows up even when he is trying to be naughty.

Some two year olds launch a more direct attack on their older sibling rival. This attack may be a string of words or it may be physical punishment. Fredricka echoed back the taunts of older children. "I don't like you. I won't even play with you. I won't be your friend." Timothy, who was equally angry at his brother Tommy was not as verbal as Fredricka. "You bad, you bad boy — you bad — banana!"

Two year olds are not always effective with their verbal barrages, but they can develop their own set of defensive or offensive weapons. Biting, scratching, pinching and missile throwing are not uncommon strategies. Most parents recognize that children can really get hurt if they are hit in the head by a rock, and throwing of things is simply not permitted. Biting seems to be another story. It is equally as disturbing to parents, but much more difficult to control. Most of the parents with biting problems told us that punishment or "biting back" techniques did not work very well. The most effective technique reported to us was ignoring the biter and paying attention to the victim. This is not the outcome that the two year old biter is attempting to bring about.

Another defensive or offensive strategy used by younger siblings is "verbal attack," crying, whining, or tantrum behavior. This technique is used most often in families that take an active stand against physical fights. The younger child learns soon enough that his cries will bring protection. Frequently the younger child begins the screaming even before he has been attacked.

A final strategy used by younger siblings is to break a treasured possession of the older sibling. From an intellectual standpoint, this is a rather advanced solution because the younger child has to recognize what his sibling values.

Some of the parents we spoke with felt very badly about emerging signs of sibling rivalry. Inevitably they blamed themselves. They hadn't done a good enough job preparing for the younger child's arrival. They weren't sensitive enough to recognize early signs of jealousy. They couldn't split themselves in two and give each child an appropriate portion of time and attention. Although this kind of self-blame is understandable it is certainly not warranted. Actually, sibling rivalry is a good sign. It shows that the children are aware of the fact that each sibling takes up some of their parents' time and attention. It also shows that the children value the time and attention of their parents. We found, in fact, that sibling rivalry is often most intense in the most child-oriented homes.

Ways of Responding to Sibling Rivalry

Every family develops its own style for handling sibling rivalry. In a family with two children each parent may unintentionally gravitate toward a different child and become that child's special confidant. Jamie was considered by both parents to be his mother's boy, while his younger brother Benjie was especially close to his father. True to form, when we left their home Jamie was looking at some pebbles with his mother and Benjie was climbing on his father's car.

The Markleys were basically a cheerful, carefree, and fun-loving family. Their usual way of handling most situations was to turn them into jokes. When Bennie insisted that his cookie was smaller than Annie's, mother responded by saying that she would feed Bennie's cookie some vitamins so that it would grow as big as Annie's. Although much of the humor went over the children's heads, they were usually able to catch the tone of their parents' remarks and would end up laughing with them.

Timothy's mother was a firm believer in talking about feelings. She felt that children were never too young to "tune into their feelings". Each day she encouraged them to talk about the things that made them feel good and the things that made them feel bad. Differences in the family were settled by talking about them. "If I stand there and let them fight and do not intervene, I am actually condoning fighting. I am saying to them, 'Go ahead, fight it out, might makes right.' No, sir. I tell my children that we talk over problems with our mouth not our fists, and you know even my two year old understands." When Allison "borrowed" Timothy's security blanket to cover her doll, Timothy came running into the room tumbling over his words. "Allison, my blanket—Allison took it, my blanket—talk about it mommy."

A few families adopted a hands off policy toward sibling rivalry. They believed that the chil-

dren would resolve their differences sooner or later if left alone. Chris' father expressed an extreme point of view along this line: "You can't pull kids apart every time they get into a fight. It's a tough world out there and they have to learn to stand up for themselves. I tell my wife, don't ever pull the kids apart unless you see blood."

In addition to these more or less unconscious styles, families actively seek out creative solutions to sibling rivalry. Some of these solutions are designed to minimize the competition among siblings for the attention of parents. Lisa and Jeffrey's mother encouraged her children to engage in parallel activities with her. One day both children might put together puzzles, each doing their own puzzle on their own brightly decorated orange crate table. The next day they might do a coloring project or play with clay. In this way both children got the special attention of their mother at the same time. This approach required a lot of planning, but based on our observation it worked well. Naturally competition and

rivalry still existed. Lisa, who certainly sensed her coloring skills were not equal to those of her four year old brother, told us as she finished a drawing, "I go slow so I can make mine more pretty."

Another systematic way to minimize competition is to establish separate times for each child to interact with parents. This is a common practice at bedtime. The children go to bed at different times, and each one gets a story or some form of special attention before going to sleep. We visited one family who had carried this idea much further and felt happy with it. Michael, the two year old, had "his time" with mother during a specified period of the day, while the two older children were at school. Shawn, who was in kindergarten, came home at 2:00 and "her time" extended for the next half hour. Later in the afternoon Billy, the eight year old, received "his time". The application of this idea seemed too rigid to us in this case, but used more flexibly the idea has merit, especially in a large family. In Betty's family each of the four children had a paper train that was moved across the wall as a reward for good behavior. The child whose train first reached the station at the end of the wall got to do something special with mother that day.

Other solutions to sibling rivalry are aimed at stopping the fighting. One of the most common techniques is to enforce the rule that children take turns enjoying special favors and privileges. At Marcie's house, for example, the children fought over saying the prayer before meals, and the most sensible solution was to take turns, even though Marcie's prayers did not make as much sense as her older brothers'. Sometimes a simple chart helps keep track of whose turn it is. The chart helps make it clear to young children that the procedure is objective and fair. Heath and Colby and Jeffrey all wanted to go grocery shopping with their father, who was not home very much. Three at a time was too much, so a chart was set up to indicate whose turn it was to accompany daddy to the store. A timer also may be appropriate for teaching children to take turns. Krista fought with her ten-year old brother over who would get to sit in daddy's chair to watch television. The problem was solved, or at least reduced in intensity, by setting a timer for ten minutes and letting the children switch seats on the bell.

Parents use various kinds of discipline to discourage fighting also. One technique is to take away the toys children are fighting over and put them up. This is a logical step, but does not seem to be too successful with a two year old, who can easily find another reason to fight if so disposed. Parents reported it was better to separate the children. This punishment is also logical in that it communicates to children that if they cannot get along they cannot play together. As Lori and Lisa's mother told us, "My girls can do without a specific toy, but it is harder to do without a companion. Within five minutes they usually have sneaked out of their rooms and are playing together quietly so I don't hear them."

It would be nice to be able to present families with the one best answer for dealing with fighting or "curing" sibling rivalry. But as is always true in child rearing there are no easy answers. Each family must work out a solution that is right for them. In the long run the best way to reduce sibling rivalry is to encourage sibling cooperation. Jeffrey, who was

four years old, had recently enlisted his two year old sister Lisa, as an ally. Together they explored the closets and hid behind the curtains. Jeffrey would turn the lights off, then they would get under the sheet and make monster and ghost noises. "Scary, mommy?" Lisa would ask. Although their mommy was not always enthusiastic about these joint endeavors, she tolerated them because they fostered a feeling of comradery between Lisa and Jeffrey.

We observed a similar pattern between Kelly and her five year old brother Kyle. They played happily in their room, filling the upper bunkbed with dolls and other toys. Their mother described how they really enjoyed washing their hands and brushing their teeth together. It was a good occasion to splash water on each other. At lunchtime they sat at a little table in the kitchen while their mother cleaned the house. Instead of eating they pushed the table back and forth, grabbed food from each other's plates and spilled their glasses of milk. The children may have been fighting, as their mother thought, but it seemed more likely to us that they were cooperating in tormenting her.

Sibling cooperation, as well as sibling rivalry, can have its drawbacks. Yet it is important to focus on the real advantages in being part of a family with more than one child. The child from a larger family has a 24 hour on-call playmate. If the on-call playmate is a baby, he can be counted on to accept rough treatment just for the joy of being with his two year old sibling. If the playmate is an older child, he is a source of stimulation, companionship and even protection. So many parents who complained about children fighting with each other on the home front told us that when other children were around, the older sibling protected the two year old.

Being part of a larger family means that children get more experience in developing social skills. Children don't just automatically learn how to play cooperatively with other children. It is very much "trial-and-error" learning. Some of the skills that children acquire in the very early years include initiating social contact with other children, laughing at each other's jokes, playing follow-the-leader games, ignoring minor hurts and falls, talking with each other, and sharing the same toys. A good place to learn these social skills is at home with sisters and brothers. It is almost a truism that the child who has had a good socialization experience in a home setting will function successfully in a new situation with children he does not know.

Twins: A Special Case

Before getting off the topic of siblings, we would like to take a brief look at some two year old twins. The interaction patterns of twins is similar to the sibling situations we have discussed, but the relationship is more intense. Generally speaking, the close contact the twins have with each other leads at an early age to both an increase in fighting and an increase in solidarity.

Chris and Michael, like many other sets of twins that have been described in the literature, were almost inseparable. On our first visit to their home Chris had a fever and fell asleep on the carpet in front of the sofa. Michael could not understand why his brother wouldn't play and continued to pull at his arms, shake him, and whisper in his ear. According to their parents, the twins either played together or fought with each other from morning to night. They had developed their own language and communicated much more with themselves than

Heath and Colby also had been inseparable at an early age, according to their mother. There had been serious fighting between them by the time they were 18 months of age. Even their older brother refused to play with them. By the age of three, however, this intense rivalry had declined. Heath and Colby were able to cooperate with each other in the manner of four or five year olds. Their social development has been accelerated.

with adults. They insisted on wearing the same thing at the same time and their parents did not dare buy a toy for one twin without finding a duplicate toy for the other. A recent incident reported by their mother typified their interlocked identities. Chris and Mike were playing in front of the house when a neighbor's child appeared on the scene and took a toy from Chris. Michael let out a blood curdling scream. It took Mrs. M. several minutes to figure out that Chris, and not Michael, had lost his toy.

The parents credited much of their success to treating the twins as distinct individuals. Each boy was encouraged to develop his own independent play style. During one of our visits Heath listened to a story record in the family room, while Colby helped his mother frost some cookies. Later we saw him riding his tricycle up and down the screened-in patio. Although the boys did spend a lot of time playing together, this selection of different activities was typical. The boys were not dressed alike and their mother did not refer to them as twins. In fact she did not like to hear other people refer to them as twins.

From our limited observation we could see that parents of twins are involved in a balancing act. On the one hand there is pressure to treat both children in the same way in order to ensure that each child is given an equal share of attention. On the other hand parents of twins feel the need to take into account individual differences. Because time and energy are limited, it is difficult to accomplish both goals, and the intense interaction pattern of twins makes the parents' job that much harder.

PLAYING WITH FRIENDS

Having an Older Friend Two year olds are usually at a perfect age for playing with older children. They are so happy with the idea of being included in the older child's play that they take on any role that is assigned.

In an imaginative play situation they are quite content to be the baby or the patient. When the other children are quite a lot older, imaginative play progresses even more smoothly. Krista, for example, had a well defined role in her 10 year old brother's peer group. While the older children pretended to be a band by playing a variety of musical instruments, Krista danced and sang. Being less inhibited she was ideal for the part.

Play with older children is not limited to imaginative play. A two year old enjoys chase games, hide'n seek activities, tumbling, tricycle riding, and any kind of jumping or climbing activities where there is an older child to play with. The fact that the two year old is less adept than the older child amuses the other child, and doesn't seem to bother the younger one. The two year old is so delighted to be riding a wheel toy with his big friend that he doesn't seem to mind the fact that the four year old covers twice the distance in half the amount of time.

Naturally, there are times when the play breaks down between the older and younger child. This is most apt to happen if the older child takes possession of a toy and completely ignores the younger child. Many manipulative toys are not designed to encourage cooperation. A battery operated helicopter, for example, only needs one "pilot". Older children usually take advantage of younger ones, giving them the less desirable toy and keeping the better one for themselves. A two year old may be satisfied playing with an inexpensive plastic airplane while the older child runs the fancy helicopter. But when imitation is not possible, and cooperation is not necessary, a two year old is likely to be left out.

When we asked parents how they felt about their two year old playing with older children, a few problems were mentioned. The most frequently expressed concern was picking up bad habits from older children. One kind of bad habit was name calling or unkind remarks. Michael picked up from the children on the block, "I don't like you. You're not my friend." In the same vein several parents mentioned that their children had started using words like "hate", "stupid", "dummy", and "baby". These are fighting words among children and become useful to the young child who is trying to substitute words for hitting and biting. Although parents are upset to hear them, they indicate that a child is progressing from physical violence to verbal aggression. Actually this concern about name calling is more characteristic of parents who do not have older children. In families with older siblings verbal assaults may be so commonplace that parents hardly notice when the two year olds joins in.

The other kind of bad habit that stood out was "cursing". Two year olds are just beginning to appreciate the attention to be gained by repeating unmentionable words. For the most part these "bad words" are innocent pooh-pooh's and pee-pee's. In Michael's neighborhood the parents were trying to squelch this kind of talk, so instead of yelling pooh-pooh and pee-pee, the children hollered "conch" and "duey", which of course meant pooh-pooh and pee-pee to anyone in the know.

These "bad words" annoy parents more because they seem stupid than because they are nasty. They are a sign to parents that the power of the peer group is growing and that in some instances its influence exceeds their own. Adele's mother was very annoyed because Adele kept saying "you bet" just like her best friend. "You're not Tina Gordon," her mother finally said in exasperation. "Well, I am Tina Gordon," Adele answered stubbornly. We know of no quick solution to this kind of problem. The best advice we can offer is to keep your sense of humor and try not to be annoyed.

The negatives that parents talked about were more than outweighed by the good effects of playing with older children. Because two year olds are great imitators, an older child can become a most effective teacher. Ginny's mother had spent many fruitless hours trying to teach Ginny how to put on her socks. Ginny resisted the lesson, "socks too hard Mommy. Ginny's a little baby." One day her three year old cousin, Barbara, spent the night. Ginny's mother was surprised the next morning when she went into the room to find Ginny on the end of the bed with both of her socks on. "Did you help Ginny with her socks?" she asked Barbara. "I putted mine on and Ginny putted hers on." Barbara answered matter of factly.

Playing with Another Two Year Old

When children play with their same age peers, the play sessions are usually less smooth than they are with older children. One of the big bug-a-boos here is sharing toys. The two year old has just got a firm handle on the concept of possessions. He recognizes that each member of the family has certain things that belong just to him. He has developed command of the language that expresses the concept of ownership. "Your briefcase," "my dog," "daddy's keys," and "my teddy bear."

Being told to share possessions is a puzzling kind of request. Why do you have to share something if it really belongs to you? Parents often urge their children to share because other children have shared with them. But how often is this true? From a two year old's perspective, other children often do not share with him, and they give every indication of wanting to keep his favorite toys. As adults we know that a shared toy eventually will be returned to its original owner, but how does a two year old know that a toy still will belong to him if he agrees to share it. The idea that possession is nine tenths of the law must seem intuitively obvious to him.

Here again we see the difference between only children and those with siblings. In a family with several children it is common to consider many of the toys joint property. This gives the children more experience in sharing, and they are more likely to share their toys with friends. This difference is only one of degree, however. There are special toys in almost every family that are the exclusive property of individual children. Brothers and sisters are not allowed to play with these special toys unless they have the owner's permission. When we visited John, for example, he grudgingly allowed his sister to play with several of the toys in his room, but she absolutely could not sit on his new motorcycle.

Between the ages of two and three many children learn to share their toys with certain friends in certain circumstances. However, it is not unusual for possessiveness to actually increase during this year. As a child has more contact with other children, his reaction may be to guard his possessions even more closely, and in addition he may begin to covet the possessions of others. In a sense being able to share represents a feeling of trust. It takes some children longer to extend this trust to their peers. Again it should be emphasized that every situation is different. A child's attitude toward sharing is affected by whose home he is in, how long he has known the other child, the personality and age of the other child, and what toy is being shared.

Even when children have progressed to the point of sharing their toys, it often happens that the toy being requested is not the toy they are willing to share. Kori discussed this dilemma with her mother in a tearful conversation:

Kori: "I don't want Jason take my Snoopy. Jason play with my Snoopy too long. Jason can play with my harmonica."

Mother: "Yes, that's a good idea. You can bring Jason your harmonica."

Kori: "Jason don't want my harmonica. Jason can play with my bubbles."

Mother: "That's a fine idea."
Kori: "Jason don't want my bubbles. I don't want to share Snoopy. I can share Snoopy with Molly. Molly gives my toys back."

As children turn three they are more likely to demonstrate selective selfishness. They now realize that one way to hurt another person or to express dislike is to deprive that person. Andy did not want one of the neighborhood boys to be allowed in his pool, and at his birthday party he told his mother that one particular girl "doesn't like cake".

The parents in our study were quite concerned about teaching their children to share. Unfortunately we found few new ideas. The rule most frequently used by parents was that whoever got a toy first had the right to keep it. This rule is crude, but it does communicate that grabbing a toy out of someone else's hand is wrong.

Sooner or later most parents try to explain why it is not nice to grab a toy. These explanations usually don't make much of an impression, judging from the dull look they inspire on the child's face. A two year old needs a concrete verbal formulation to catch the meaning of the idea. Mary's mother seemed to have hit on a good one. When a fight broke out over a toy she tried to find out who the trespasser was by referring to him as the grouch. "Who's the grouch now? Bev, you're the grouch — Robbie already had the cement mixer. Come on grouch. Let's find you another toy." The children soon learned how the grouch was determined and that everyone was the grouch at one time or another. The verbal ritual of being labeled the grouch communicated in a non-punitive way, one of the basic rules of sharing.

Mary's mother had introduced another verbal formula at an early age that facilitated sharing. At the dinner table food often was divided and distributed by saying "One for Mary, One for Mommy, and One for Daddy". This formula was repeated in diverse settings, such as rolling a ball back and forth and saying "One for Mommy...One for Mary." By the age of two Mary showed interest in dividing her toys among her friends the same way. The magic of simple counting helped overcome her tendency to hoard possessions.

Matthew's mother suggested an interesting technique to us. Many families allow a child to take one toy when they go out. This toy can be used in the car and also at a friend's house. Matthew's mother reversed the idea. She taught Matthew to take one of his toys just for the friend to play with. In this way Matthew was able to initiate the sharing by offering a toy to the host child, rather than the usual procedure of waiting for the largesse of the host to materialize. Imagine how much less threatened the host child must feel when his guest immediately gives him a new toy to play with. The idea is comparable to bringing flowers or wine when invited to dinner, a token of gratitude in advance.

Terri's mother was really fond of having children come to play. Her strategy was to involve the children in a game or activity where sharing was less likely to be a problem. Frequently she introduced some sort of craft or cooking activity in which the children could cooperate. Other times she encouraged activities in which the children could imitate each other. The most successful activities were highly physical. The house had a large screened-in porch directly off the kitchen that could be filled with appropriate equipment. Some days she placed a wading pool on the porch and let the children play in the water. Some days she invited the children to bring their tricycles over. Her favorite setup was an old mattress, several cartons of different sizes, and some old sheets, blankets and pillows. The children climbed in and on the cartons, jumped on the mattress and pillows, crawled under the sheets and blankets, and generally had a wild time.

Parents sometimes are concerned about the wild behavior of a two year old peer group. Even when only two children get together, their play quite often appears to be regressive. Adele had gone beyond the stage of pulling everything off the shelves and her room stayed reasonably neat. When her friend Yvonne came over to play, her mother saw no reason not to let the children play by themselves in Adele's room. She was thoroughly dismayed when she walked into the room several minutes later and found the place in a shambles. All the toys were out of the toy box, books off the shelf, clothes out of the drawers, and even the bed clothes were off the bed.

Other kinds of play that parents consider regressive include chasing games, snatch away the toy games, shouting, throwing things, raucous laughter, and knocking all sorts of things over. It is probably a mistake to consider this type of spontaneous interaction between two year olds as regressive play. What is happening is that the two year olds are attempting to involve each other in a game. They are not sophisticated enough to think up a complicated game so they rely on activities that are guaranteed to produce social interaction. In actuality the noisy rambunctious pair of two year olds who are making a mess of the house are taking an important step toward learning social skills.

STYLES OF PLAYING

Each child's personality and play style is unique, but it is common for first born children to be somewhat domineering between the ages of two and three, especially if their parents are the kind that reason and compromise with them. These children are used to having their ideas treated with respect within the family and they expect peers to do the same. We visited several families in which first born children between 2½ and 3 were trying to direct three and four year old children. Michael, for example, organized the peer group's imaginative play around a hospital theme, casting himself in the principal role. He became upset if the neighbor children wanted to play by themselves instead of playing with him. Beverly assumed her mother's role of helping the peer group do arts and crafts projects. Her mother was proud of Beverly's leadership ability but cringed at her bossiness: "Don't color that way, Lisa—All right, time to stop coloring—Put your crayons away right now."

This bossiness may be received surprisingly well by the other children. Lacking social cohesion, the peer group tends to welcome someone who can get things organized, and the bossy commands don't really have much sting when they come from another child.

Of course, later born children can develop a domineering play style also. We found families in which the second child had been encouraged to be more assertive because the parents had changed their minds about discipline. They felt they had been too strict with their first child and so were allowing the second child more leeway to argue with them and to stretch the rules. Then there is the situation in which the youngest child is especially indulged because he is the last baby in the family.

In general, children between the ages of two and three are just beginning to define their style of playing with peers and they begin by transferring the style they have developed within the family.

As a member of an extended family, Rocheda had developed an excellent reservoir of social skills. During our visit Rocheda's mother took out the vacuum cleaner so that we could see how well Rocheda had learned to push it around. Unfortunately, her cousin Eddie was also interested in the vacuum cleaner and managed to get to it first. The first strategy Rocheda tried for retrieving the vacuum cleaner was a polite request. It didn't work. Next, she tried a kiss—still no success. Finally, she gave her cousin a good shove and yanked the vacuum out of his hand.

Although every child brings his own style to a play situation, we found a common pattern in the evolution of peer group relationships. At first the two year old tends to be unusually passive in a new peer group. The child takes the role of onlooker, imitator, and follower. During this phase parents may be distressed that their child lets himself be pushed around. Jenny's mother told us, "Jenny is the smallest child in the neighborhood, and the other kids were always hitting her and taking away her toys. Finally I had to tell her to hit them back."

One of the reasons two year olds get into fights is that they find it difficult to organize their play. Organization requires both responsive leaders and responsible followers. Two year olds do not fit easily into either role. The dominant children have trouble communicating their plans and they are basically tyrannical. The more passive children have trouble seeing any sense in the largely unintelligible plans of the "leaders", and they are expert at sabotaging these plans by teasing or withdrawing. In these circumstances physical games of imitation are a natural peer group activity. They require little sharing and almost no social organization.

Many parents reported to us that their two year old's social play was more sophisticated when playing with a single friend instead of a group of peers. Two children who know each other well are more likely to have settled on a stable interaction pattern, with one child being more of a leader and the other child more of a follower. When both children have a forceful, bossy style of play, this process of establishing social roles can take a long time.

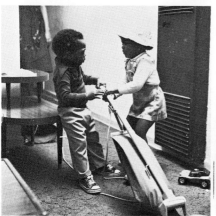

Whether or not parents urge their two year olds to defend themselves, most children begin to assert themselves as they become more familiar with a group of children. This self-assertion takes many different forms: physical violence, teasing, bribing, commanding, and sometimes even persuading.

Often children become unusually assertive just as they were unusually passive earlier. Jenny's mother related that after Jenny started asserting her rights, there was a constant struggle over toys. She found it necessary to intervene almost continually when two or three friends were playing in Jenny's room.

Eventually some kind of balance is struck as the members of the group develop a stable pattern of interaction. In the case of Jenny's peer group it took about three months. Parents can play an important role in helping children progress through this sequence by offering suggestions and explanations. Wherever possible, they should avoid overreacting if their child appears either too timid or too aggressive. Joining the peer group is both exciting and frightening for most two year olds and it takes time for them to find their place.

As in other aspects of child rearing parents need to recognize that children are different and do not need the same kinds of social experiences. Some children enjoy watching from the sidelines, or playing along side another child, but do not want to join in the noisy activity of the peer group. At a birthday party Lori, who is basically a gentle, non-aggressive child, retreated into a corner and played quietly until the party ended. "I don't want a lot of screaming kids at my birthday party," she informed her mother.

GROUP EXPERIENCE

Choosing the Right Setting

Many families must put their young children in a child care facility because there is no adult at home during the day to take care of them. Other families choose to send two year olds to nursery school or a play group because they feel the children need the experience. We found that the parents in our study expressed two contrasting points of view about the best environment for children between the ages of two and three. According to one school of thought two year olds are too young for cooperative play or for directed activity and should be allowed to spend their time in a relaxed climate playing with toys and exploring the things around them. The role of the adult is primarily to make certain that the children are safe and happy. The contrasting philosophy is based on the belief that two year olds are ready for a more structured environment and can benefit from carefully planned experiences and direct teaching.

It seems to us that both of these philosophies are valid. Two year olds need a predictable environment in which they feel emotionally secure and are free to set their own direction and pace for learning. At the same time two year olds can benefit from a stimulating environment that is based on careful planning, specialized materials and exposure to a variety of children and adults. Ideally group settings for young children should combine the qualities of both environments. They should offer the advantages of both a home and a school.

In our experience, however, many group child care facilities do not approach this ideal. They have neither the atmosphere of a good home nor the planning of a good school. Our impression is that this situation will not change unless a much higher level of resources is available to day care centers.

In visiting day care centers we were impressed by the ability of the children to regulate their behavior in the classroom. The children were well adjusted to the large group setting. They sat quietly at tables waiting for instructions, went to the bathroom in orderly fashion, and ate their food with restraint. However, they did not seem very happy about it, and as soon as we tried to start an informal conversation or game with one child, we were inundated by other children seeking some of our attention. This frantic scramble for attention suggests that a highly structured situation does not meet the needs of children.

Two year old children who are used to staying at home may have difficulty adjusting to a large group environment. Many of the parents in our study reported that their two year olds begged to go to school like their older siblings, but after having tried it, they wanted no more of it. Jodi's case was a bit extreme but not atypical. She insisted on going to school, but as soon as her mother left, Jodi crawled out the window in order to escape. Trying another school, Jodi's mother found that she had to carry Jodi kicking and screaming to the car every morning. At pick-up time Jodi was all smiles and claimed to have had a fine day at school.

Jodi's case illustrates the fact that many two year olds do want contact with other children. They want both the social experience and the feeling of expanding their horizons beyond the home. Her behavior also demonstrates, however, the fact that a large group setting is often overwhelming for two year olds who have been cared for in a home environment.

In order to combine the qualities of home and school, we feel it is highly desirable to organize day care, nursery school, and other group experiences for two year olds in terms of small groups. A small group might consist of five to ten children. Here are some additional features that seem important to us in choosing a group setting for two year olds:

- The adults who work with the children are loving, enthusiastic and energetic. They have a good sense of timing and are able to suggest a new activity or change in locale before a crisis happens. They call all the children by name, bend down to their level when they speak with them, and talk with each child about the "important things" like what they are wearing, what is happening at home or what they did yesterday. They also have the capacity of seeing what is going on in all four corners of the room simultaneously.

- The center has places set up for different types of activities. There is a place for pretend play, a place for motor activities, a place for arts and crafts, a place for reading and listening, and a place for constructing things. There is also a fenced-in place for outdoor play. The center is equipped with safe and intact materials that encourage these different kinds of activities. Play material is within reach of the children.

- The daily schedule provides some time for free play and some time for planned activity. The planned activities are very simple; circle games, exercises on the mat, marching to music, listening to a story, tearing and pasting bits of paper, going for a walk, learning a finger play. Teachers begin the day by describing what is going to happen, and end the day by summarizing what has happened. Certain activities are repeated on a daily basis to provide the children with a sense of time and sequence.

- Parents are an integral part of program planning and are frequent visitors to the center.

- There is at least one adult for every five two to three year olds.

A Case Study

We had the opportunity to accompany Kori one day when she attended the group setting her parents had arranged. The group met for part of the day in the home of a lady who served as the teacher. The group was quite small, only four children, and this allowed the teacher to give a lot of individual attention to children when they needed it. Certain activities were planned, but because of the smallness of the group it was easy to deviate from these plans, to combine informality with structured activities.

We were struck by the fragility of the group's social cohesion. The children faded in and out of the group, now joining in with enthusiasm, now withdrawing in apprehension. Although the children seemed to thoroughly enjoy their day, there was relief when it was over. Again the smallness of the group enabled the teacher to respond to this ambivalence with sensitivity. Here is a description of our visit:

When Kori arrived, Lisa was climbing up and down the stairs while Molly and Jason were playing in the basement inside a large box. Kori stood watching for several moments while Jason and Molly followed each other inside the "boat" shouting, "Hurry, the water is coming, the water is coming." Suddenly Jason jumped out of the box asking, "Where are the police?" Molly continued to shout, "Water is coming. Got to go on the other boats." The "other boats" were two rocking horses in the corner of the room. For several minutes Jason and Molly ran back and forth from box to horses giggling contagiously and shouting out bits of dialogue, "boats going faster", "water is coming down on me", "let's go riding in a boat", "row row your boat".

Marie, the play group teacher, prepared some colored paste which could be spread with a paint brush, and gave Lisa colored paper, a brush, the paints, a box of buttons, egg carton sections and small bits of junk. Lisa took the brush and became interested in transferring the paste to the paper. She was not at all interested in the product she was creating and was quite unconcerned when the paper became oversaturated and the paste spread onto the table.

Kori was watching intently, her attention vacillating back and forth between the two groups. She had not let go of her security objects, Raggedy Ann, and a blanket called Fringe. Finally Marie persuaded Kori to join Lisa at the little table, and gave Kori her own paste, brush and paper. In marked contrast to Lisa, Kori began the task by making three puddles of paste in the center of her paper. She gazed at the globs for a few seconds, her fists clenched in a characteristic gesture of heightened excitement. At this point Lisa snatched away Kori's paste and Kori responded with a kind of "shout-whine". Marie gave Lisa her own paste, and both girls went back to the activity. Lisa saturated a second piece of paper, and with some help from Marie, stuck two buttons on top of the paper. Her behavior at this point became less mature and within a few seconds she splashed the paste on the table, rubbed her pasty hands on her face and across Marie's skirt, and threw a small cake pan at Marie.

Jason and Molly came over to the table to see what was going on. Marie invited them both to make their own paste collage. She explained that they were using paste and not paint and that they could stick things on it. Jason stuck a button on Kori's painting. Kori objected mildly but then took up the task. Apparently Kori had been so involved in spreading the paste prior to Jason's arrival that she hadn't explored the possibility of placing buttons on the paste. Jason and Molly worked at their collages for a short time. Jason was especially interested in where the collage would hang after it was finished. He went around the room identifying all of the art work and naming the artist.

Marie suggested that it was time to go upstairs and pop some popcorn. All four children responded to the suggestion by going to the stairs. Molly was in the lead with Jason running a close second. Kori followed cautiously behind, while Lisa got distracted by her collage which was drying on the stairs. Marie explained that it had to stay there for a while or the paste would drip off. She handled a minor burst of temper with a distracting hug and went upstairs to prepare for the popcorn popping.

All four children sat on stools around the stove as Marie demonstrated the popcorn making steps. Lisa kept touching the stove despite Marie's admonition but finally responded to a firm "no" as they sat around the table eating popcorn. Marie repeated the popcorn making steps. Molly told Marie she had found a seed. Marie explained that it was called a kernel. When Marie asked her a few minutes later what it was called, she said, "I don't know" and Jason, who appeared to be completely absorbed in comparing his popcorn supply with Kori's helped out with the word, "kernel".

Marie asked the children if they would like to go for a walk. Molly and Jason exchanged some banter. It's too cold; it is not cold outside; it's a little bit hot. Marie asked Kori how she felt about the walk. Kori answered, "It's not too cold outside — I wanta go for a walk." This seemed to be the deciding vote, and after everyone promised not to walk in the puddles, Marie put on the jackets, gave them each a cabbage leaf, and out they went.

The agreed upon destination of the walk was the rabbit hutches, but the children seemed to be more concerned about what they were finding along the way than where they were going. The first intriguing stopping off place was a sewer. Jason discovered the sewer first, and Marie took advantage of his obvious interest to present a mini lesson on melting snow. Kori listened intently and even when the other children had gone off to new things, she stood on the sewer clutching Fringe and Raggedy Ann and watching the falling of water. The next major stopping off place on the walk was a plank of wood that spanned the flooded gutter in front of one of the houses. Jason said, "Look, a bridge," and Molly and Jason followed each other from one side to the other. Kori watched for a while and then announced, "I go on the bridge" and walked slowly back and forth. Molly and Jason stood aside as if recognizing that this was an important feat for Kori. At this point Lisa began to squeal and Marie offered to help her get across. Lisa walked sideways and after a few seconds let go of Marie's hand and made it back and forth.

It took some urging from Marie to get the children away from the bridge. Kori took the lead, shouting "run, run, run" but Jason and Molly were out front in a few seconds. Their run was interrupted by a couple of garbage cans and Marie had to do some more persuading to get them to continue the walk.

Once at their destination Jason, Molly and Kori fed the rabbits. Kori stuck the cabbage through the fence, keeping a safe distance between her fingers and the rabbit's teeth. Molly fed the rabbit quickly and raced to the top of a little play house chanting. "I'm the king of the castle and you're the dirty rascal." Jason took several minutes to join Molly as he seemed to be quite involved in sticking the cabbage in the rabbit's mouth. Lisa chewed on her piece of cabbage as she watched the other children.

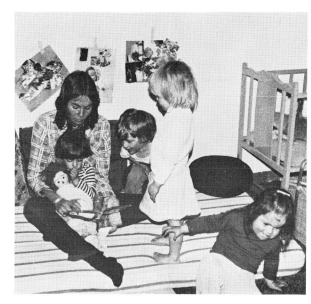

After all four of the children climbed to the top of the play house Marie suggested that it was time to walk home. The home trip involved the same stopping off places. This time Lisa went on the bridge with no help but fell in the middle and landed on her back in the puddle. Her crying was short lived, but she did cling to Marie's hand for the rest of the trip home.

After changing out of wet clothes the children went downstairs and began free play. For a few seconds Kori, Jason and Molly played together with some Fisher Price miniatures. Then Kori put her arms rather possessively around a playschool toy and made a kind of snarling sound when Jason tried to touch it. At this point Marie asked the children if they would like to read the jumping bean story. Kori sat herself on Marie's lap while Jason and Molly sat on either side. (Lisa was playing by herself with a stuffed toy.) Kori appeared to be listening intently to the story pointing out the different illustrations. Molly and Jason were more interested in being jumping beans but listened to the appropriate cues in the story.

"Time to clean up." Marie announced as the children asked for one more story. Cleaning up met with no resistance. This time Kori took the lead, systematically picking up each toy and putting it back in its place. Lisa helped put some puzzle pieces in a box but had some problem differentiating between putting the toys away and taking them out again.

When the clean up was accomplished, Marie announced that it was exercise time. Kori, after her burst of energy in the clean up chore, stood with thumb in mouth as Jason and Molly did forward and backward somersaults on the mat. When Marie suggested circle games, Kori was ready to play again. Ring around a Rosie went very well. Kori knew all the words and continued to sing even when Jason and Molly got so interested in the "all fall down" part that they went from singing to shouting.

It was lunch time. Molly was not happy when she found that her lunch consisted of yogurt and strawberries. After some maneuvering Marie managed a trade between Jason and Molly. Lisa was obviously tired by now. She broke her sandwich into bits, stood at her place, banged on the table, and finally dissolved into tears. Marie took Lisa upstairs and she went to sleep without protest. Jason had a cookie in his lunch box and Marie divided it into three pieces to share among the children. Jason ate his piece and a piece of Molly's. Marie averted a crisis by instructing Jason to share his banana with Molly.

Following lunch Marie changed diapers, washed faces and reviewed the morning events, letting the children tell parts of the story. The activity ended abruptly when Molly's mother arrived. Molly clung to her mother and started to whine. Her mother's gentle and loving response turned the whine into a cry. It was as if Molly had been on her best behavior all morning, but now she was exhausted and in the safety of her mother's arms she was expressing her exhaustion through her tears. Jason was watching Molly's reaction. Marie sat Jason in her lap, and he put his thumb in his mouth. Kori too had been watching Molly's performance and smiled in relief as her mother arrived to take her home.

Chapter III—Increased Awareness

Self-Awareness 49
Relating To Others 53
   Within the Family 53
   Beyond the Immediate Family 57
New Discoveries 59
   Space, time, and number 59
   New ideas about life 61
Summary 64

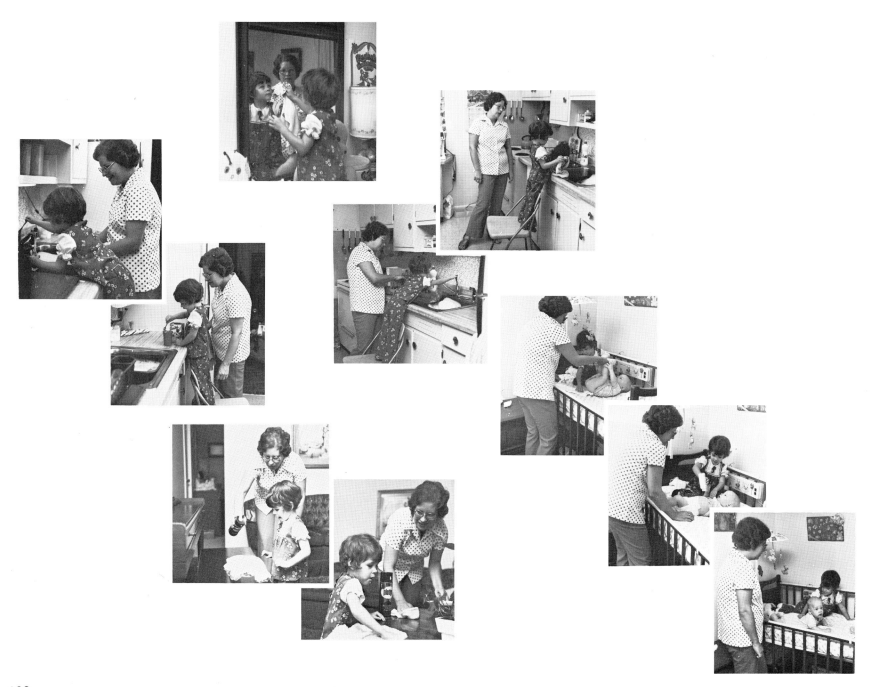

Chapter III
Increased Awareness

We asked parents in a preliminary questionnaire to describe the most enjoyable experiences they had had with their two year old. The answers fell into three categories. In the first category parents described special moments in which their child expressed empathy, kindness, or compassion:

"When we visited Matthew's great grandmother who is 91 years old, Matthew showed a particular kindness for her. As we left to get into the car, he let go of my hand and reached for her. At the same time he looked up at her and said, 'a kiss, a hug!'"

In the second category of responses parents expressed delight with their child's mastery of language:

"The most enjoyable experience I have had is communication with my child — being able to communicate more and more one to the other."

In the third category of responses parents described their child's manifest ability to learn:

"We made a visit to the Miami Seaquarium. Kim was delighted with the fish exhibits and the whale show. It was such a pleasure watching her learn new things."

Clearly the experiences that delighted parents most were related to new and emerging capacities of the two year old. In this chapter we will discuss these emerging capacities under three headings: self-awareness, relating to others, and new discoveries.

SELF-AWARENESS

"Now I am a boy," Matthew told his mother as he pulled on a new pair of underpants. "Now I am a baby," he announced a little later when his naptime diaper was put on.

Although many children may not be as expressive as Matthew, the transition from babyhood to childhood is not accomplished without detours and backtracking. At one moment the two year old refuses his father's hand as he mounts a flight of stairs or walks along a busy street. A moment later he is afraid of stepping over a crack in the sidewalk and asks his father to carry him. It is natural for a two year old to feel ambivalent about growing up. Growing up involves giving up the comforts and luxuries of babyhood. Furthermore, along with greater privileges come greater expectations.

A part of a two year old's struggle to grow up is reflected in a stubborn determination to do things by himself. This determination is so strong at times that parents get a feeling of rejection. In a sense, this feeling is justified. In his intense desire to establish himself as a separate person with a mind and purpose of his own, the two year old may reject parental assistance even when he needs it. Because each new accomplishment adds to his feeling of power and control, he is desperate to master new things.

Timothy was in the process of opening up his father's tool box. It was a tricky catch and the latch kept snapping back in the final stage of the operation. His frustration made him feel inept, and his mother finally gave in to the temptation to help him. "I do it myself," Timothy snapped as he pulled the box away from his mother. Timothy's refusal to let his mother help demonstrated the fact that opening the box by himself was much more important to Timothy than getting at the contents.

In a somewhat similar incident Merilee was testing her ability to run up the playground slide. After several unsuccessful attempts Merilee seemed frustrated and her mother offered to help. "No," Merilee insisted, "I don't want to run up the slide."

This kind of rationalization helped Merilee maintain her self-image. Her mother recognized that running up the slide by yourself was what counted, not actually reaching the top, and so she let the matter drop.

Predictably, the two year old is not very good at handling teasing. Any kind of teasing serves as a threat to this newly developed and somewhat fragile self-image. When Richard's dad suggested kiddingly that Richard was a little baby, the reaction was immediate. "I not a baby, I a big boy, and I can't like that."

An important indication of the two year old's emerging sense of self is an increasing ability to describe and express feelings. The two year olds in our study displayed a wide range of emotional reactions — love, joy, pride, happiness, shyness, anger, jealousy. Sometimes parents inferred these feelings from their child's behavior. At other times the two year olds expressed their feelings in words.

Many of our parents described with delight how their two year old would give them a spontaneous hug and say, "I love you." Christopher's mother describes her reaction to Christopher's words of endearment. "No matter how ornery or bull headed that son of mine can get, when he says, 'mommy, I love you really,' I just melt."

Closely related to these expressions of open affection are the two year olds expressions of joy. "It is such a beautiful day," exclaimed Zachary as he and his mother chased a butterfly across the backyard. Often the two year old's expression of joy is associated with a sense of accomplishment. Wendy sang out loud as she swung higher and higher on the playground. "I swinging, I swinging, I swinging, I so happy swinging."

Going along with this increased capacity to show love and joy is a new capacity for empathy. Several of our parents were amazed and delighted at their two year olds concern with the problems of other people. Jody reacted to a story about Rodriguez the Lion, whom nobody wanted to play with, by telling her mother that if Rodriguez arrived on her street, she would play with him. Kori scolded the husky dogs in a television program for pushing Snoopy around. Chad explained to the baby in his mommy's tummy, "If you come out of there, I'll let you play with my toys." Merilee responded to the televised plight of some flood victims by offering to share her blankets.

Related to the ability to express emotion is a greater concern about the feelings of their parents. When Marcie's mother stubbed her toe, there were tears in Marcie's eyes. When Allison accidently broke the vase, she asked her mother plaintively, "did I make you sad?" Janet was just gaining enough control to learn how to use the toilet. Her mother came back from a shopping expedition and was greeted at the door by a very proud daughter. "Feel my pants. Are you happy mommy?"

Although parents are often troubled by it, it is not surprising to find that two year olds are as open about their negative feelings as they are about their good feelings. Kelly responded to her mother's refusal to let her carry a piece of cake on a paper plate

by shouting, "Darn you — you stupid, stupid, stupid." Eddie, angered by his father's refusal to let him play with the toaster, stamped his foot and declared, "I hate you bad!" Other negative feelings that two year olds expressed were jealousy, sadness, and fear. "Julie shut me out, Julie make me sad,"

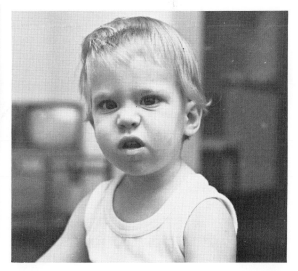

Zachary complained when his sister shut the door to her room. Jodi came running into her mother's room after watching a television cartoon, "Mommy, that T.V. makes my tummy shake."

The expression of good and bad feelings by two year olds is an outgrowth of their emerging self-awareness. Another outgrowth of self-awareness is an increased ability to identify likes and dislikes. "I want to try that," said Kori to her Nana as she pointed to some iced coffee. "You won't like it Kori," Nana explained, "it has a bitter taste." "I want to try that," Kori insisted a little more firmly. "Ok, try it," Nana agreed, "take a little taste," Kori tried it. "I don't like Nana's coffee. I like Daddy's tea better."

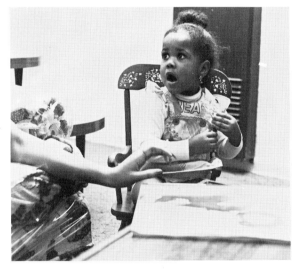

As the two year old increases his awareness of what he likes and what he doesn't like, he becomes increasingly concerned about getting what he wants and keeping it. Two year olds are like other people in that their self-image is sustained partly by possessions. Being less sure of themselves, their possessiveness is more rigid and shrill. Two year olds are possessive about their toys, their clothes, their house, and their parents.

For a two year old possessions offer stability rather than status. For example, several parents told us their children reacted negatively when the family car was traded in for a new one. The new car was fancier, but the old car was familiar. Moving to a new house, or even changing the furniture in the old house, was upsetting to some children. "I don't want you take down my crib," Matthew insisted, even though he hadn't slept in his crib for months. "I don't want new shoes," Heath screamed, holding on desperately to a beat up pair of sneakers. Andrew cried for an hour when the dead tree behind their house was cut down.

Any object, whether it is a possession or not, can acquire emotional significance. In fact, some objects take on so much meaning that they seem to become symbols. For many children vehicles of all types come to symbolize the feeling of mastery, of being in control. Birthday cakes may become symbolic of happiness or security. We found the birthday cake ritual repeated over and over in different contexts. A feeling of fear may be symbolized by a cave, a cage, or a jail, i.e. the places where dangerous animals and people are to be found. We cannot be sure these symbols really exist for two year olds, but we think it is fun to consider the idea. Parents can watch their children to see if certain objects recur in imaginative play, block constructions, drawings, and conversations.

The most important possessions for two year olds are the people who surround them, their families. A central part of their self-awareness is a recognition that they belong to a family. One way two year olds demonstrate this new awareness is to list all the family members at every opportunity. When recalling a recent trip to Disney World, Heather talked little about what actually happened. "Heather, and Mommy and Daddy, and Grandma and Grandpa and Aunt Susan went in the car. Heather and Mommy and Daddy and Grandma and Grandpa and Aunt Susan ate pancakes in the hotel."

Names are a special part of each person's self-image. Two year olds, who are just beginning to see themselves as separate people, treat their names as treasured objects. "That's my K," Kori asserted when she found her initials on a Kellogg's box. "T is

for Terry," insisted Terry whenever he saw a capital T. "That man not named Erik," Erik yelled when informed of Erik Severeid's name.

The listing of family members is not limited to the child's own family. As soon as the child grasps the concept of people belonging in a family he begins to ask questions about other mommies and daddies. In fact the family is such an important organizing principle that it is extended to all forms of life, and even to inanimate objects. Jean went through a period where she searched for a mommy and a daddy for every animal in her story book. Lori saw some baby kittens in the pet store and told the owner that the kittens were crying for their mommy. Cathy arranged her Fisher Price characters in groups of three. "This mommy, and this daddy, and this baby go over here. This mommy and daddy and this baby go on the other side."

Kori began a dialogue with a big raisin and a little raisin that she found in her cereal. "This is the mommy raisin," she told her mother.

"I want to go outside and play."
"You can't go outside — it's too cold."
"I want to play in the cold."

Kori resolved the disagreement quite suddenly, "Baby's all gone. I ate the baby raisin."

More significant than the two year old's naming of the family members is his gradual recognition of the functions that a family serves. For the two year old a family serves a double function. On the one hand it provides the two year old with opportunities to establish and express his autonomy. On the other hand it provides a base of security where his needs for dependency are recognized.

Several parents in our study gave fairly parallel descriptions of their child's first stay with a relative. With the exception of awakening during the night, the children were described as being perfect angels, no hassles, no temper tantrums, no whining and no defiance. From the moment the children got home, however, the spell of good behavior came to an abrupt halt. The children were described as being ornery, defiant and downright stubborn. At the same time they were reverting to really babyish behavior, whining, asking to be carried, and even demanding a bottle. "Grandma just spoiled her rotten," one mother complained. It would probably be more accurate to describe this behavior as a normal reaction to a temporary loss of home. Home is the place where children express a double valance. On the one hand they enjoy the security provided by loving parents. On the other hand they test out the limits of their autonomy. Just as a person who loses a wallet checks on the contents when the wallet is found, the child who has been away from his parents tests out the ingredients of home.

RELATING TO OTHERS

Within the Family

The period from two to three years is frequently labeled the "terrible twos" in recognition of the unpredictable and seemingly uncontrollable behavior of so many two year olds. At one moment the youngster is delighting the family with his imaginative play and his humorous antics. At the next moment he is in the throes of a full fledged tantrum,

shouting, crying, kicking his legs and beating his fists on the floor. A problem as trivial as a stuck zipper or a "no" to a stick of chewing gum may set off this display of temper.

Such a stereotypical description needs to be qualified immediately in at least three ways. First, this kind of erratic behavior nearly always occurs in a familiar social setting. It is most likely when children are within the family. Faced with a new environment, such as a new babysitter, day care center, or peer group, two year olds tend to be passive and cautious.

Second, the temper tantrum is only one of a whole range of tactics that two year olds develop as a means of asserting themselves in a social situation. These techniques include arguing, rationalizing, threatening, ordering, teasing, whining, hitting, kissing, hugging, making cute faces, and many other more subtle variations that are too hard to name. Just as the second year of life is characterized by a proliferation of new skills for exploring the environment, the third year is witness to an explosion of social skills. Many of these skills existed earlier in a nascent form, but now they become fully

recognizable. The two year old's emerging self-awareness, his new facility with language, his refined ability to imitate other people, his awareness that parents are distinct individuals, the combination of these and other factors enables the two year old to interact within the family on a new plane.

Third, although nearly all two year olds have temper tantrums, there are striking differences between children. Each child creates his own blend of social skills and develops his own preferred style. Some two year olds excel in being argumentative and defiant. Some are especially good at manipulating parents with hugs and kisses. Some make excuses and invent imaginary scapegoats. Some are whiners.

Having made these qualifications, there still remains a kernel of truth in the description of this year as the "terrible twos." The two year old is developing a set of strategies to control parents, while parents are countering with a set of strategies to control the two year old. Frequently, there is a clash, and sometimes the battles do become terrible for both parties.

For a child who has just turned two the most prominent technique for self-assertion is likely to be a defiant "no." Children discover that a "no" has power, and they use it at every opportunity.

"Tommy, would you like to come to the drugstore with Daddy and me?"

"No, don't wanna."

"You can pick out a birthday card to send Pop-Pop."

"No, don't wanna."

"Okay, then stay here with Jeffrey."

(Tommy burst into tears.) "Me go drugstore Mommy, Daddy."

Tommy said "no" even though he really wanted to say "yes." His behavior seems perverse unless we interpret it as an experiment. Tommy was putting his power to say "no" to the test, seeing how far it would carry him. This kind of testing behavior is characteristic of every new interpersonal skill that a two year old develops. Kori, for example, developed a string of imaginary characters who provided a ready made excuse for resisting parental requests. "Would you like to help me put away your toys so that we'll be ready to go out when Daddy comes?" her mother asked. "No, I can't," Kori explained. "I have to look after Aki and her sisters and all the little babies." Amy, who discovered that she got special consideration because of a headache, started to develop stomach aches, leg aches, and back aches. Even peas were refused at dinner because "they hurt my mouth."

Two year olds practice new social skills just like any other new skill they develop. However, it would be wrong to assume that the children are only involved in testing their ability to manipulate parents. When two year old children assert themselves, regardless of the technique, there usually is some genuine emotion involved.

Pamela's family mentioned in their questionnaire that the thing they could not stand about Pamela was her incessant whining. Sure enough, as soon as we got to the house, Pamela began whining for a cookie. Her mother explained that she could not have a cookie because it was too close to lunch. Pamela continued to whine. Finally her mother could not stand it anymore and gave Pamela a piece of cookie.

It seemed to us that Pamela's mother had been manipulated into breaking her own rule about eating snacks. But this manipulation is only part of the story. It also seemed to us that Pamela could not understand the reason for prohibiting cookies before lunch and, therefore, she had a genuine emotional response of sadness. From her point of view she had a good reason to be whiny and sad.

Pamela's mother was placed in a dilemma. If she gave into the whining, she was encouraging more manipulative behavior of this kind in the future. On the other hand, if she ignored the whining and did not give in, she was discouraging honest emotional expression in the future. One message was "I'll break my rule if you whine;" the other message was "don't tell me about it if you feel sad." Neither choice is really satisfactory.

Actually we have presented an example that is relatively one sided. Many parents would have refused to give Pamela the cookie. But what if Pamela had been whining for some nutritious snack, or had been trying to get her mother to stop talking to us and mix some paint. In real life two year olds often express reasonable requests in unreasonable ways. Of course, one can take the position that whining never should be responded to, but this seems unfair to us. It is like saying to the child, "find some nice way to express your bad feelings."

It sometimes is suggested that parents can sympathize with a child's feeling and refuse a request at the same time. "I know you're feeling sad but I'm not going to give you a cookie until after lunch." In theory this approach meets the needs of both parents and children. In practice, however, it is harder to pull off than it sounds. Other options include compromising, trying to explain, or distracting. Our intent here is not to describe all the options available to parents, but to emphasize the complexity of these situations and to reassure parents that there are no pat solutions.

139

Temper tantrums are even more disconcerting than whining. Timothy's mother told us about a recent tantrum that had occurred at a park. Like many two year olds, Timothy loved exploring the playground equipment at parks. As a special treat they had stopped at a new park on their way downtown. After 15 or 20 minutes Timothy's mother told Timothy it was time to leave and go shopping. His response was "I don't wanna," and when she took his hand, he suddenly pulled away, threw himself on the ground and started to scream. "That tantrum really wasn't too bad," Timothy's mother went on. "Nobody else was near us so I didn't feel embarrassed. I ignored Timothy's screaming, just picked him up and put him in the car. But when he pulls that kind of trick in the grocery store or a restaurant, I don't know what to do."

Like Pamela, there was both manipulation and genuine emotion in Timothy's behavior. He had learned from previous experience that he sometimes got his way by screaming. At the same time he was genuinely angry because he could not understand why it was necessary to leave the park. Again, we have selected an example in which most parents would not respond to the temper tantrum. But what if Timothy had lost his temper because he could not complete a puzzle or because his ice cream cone fell on the ground? In this kind of situation many parents would respond to the child's expression of frustration and rage. They would offer to help with the puzzle or they would buy another ice cream cone. Each situation is different. Sometimes we refuse to be manipulated, sometimes we respond to the child's feelings, and sometimes we try to do both.

Each new social skill a two year old develops can run the gamut from entertaining to infuriating. Chad's mother, for example, could not help but laugh at Chad's attempt to threaten her. When she told him there would be no dessert until he finished every bit of his meat, he looked her straight in the eye and said, "there will be tears." On the other hand, when Beverly threatened her mother in a similar situation by saying, "I hate you," there was no laughing.

Many children experiment at some point with hitting their parents as an assertive technique. As in Jed's family this behavior may seem cute at first. It was funny to see Jed trying to stand up to his father by slapping ineffectually at his leg. However, eventually he began to hit his father and uncles in the face when they didn't see things his way. This kind of hitting made them angry, and they struck back at Jed.

Just as the toddler is faced with the problem of figuring out when and where exploration is allowed, the two year old has to learn when and how to use new social skills. It is a problem of discrimination. Each technique has its place and is acceptable at times. The fact that parents respond differently in different situations makes it more difficult for children to learn how to behave. But in reality social interaction is very complicated. It is not governed by a set of straightforward and simplistic rules.

So far we have been talking about some of the negative ways that two year olds assert themselves. More positive techniques also are developed for relating to parents. A please, a hug, a kiss, or a little flattery go a long way toward keeping parents "in line." A particularly effective strategy that some two year olds learn is "I'm sorry." Shawn had been playing with the water pump, although he knew full well that it was off bounds. Just as his mother was about to scold him, Shawn looked up with a most innocent expression, "I sorry, you angry Mommy?" Heather, who was also good at manipulating her parents, had her own "behavioral modification" system for keeping her father in line. When her father was doing things her way, she gave him lots of hugs and kisses. When her father "misbehaved," she let him give her a goodnight kiss and then wiped it away with her sheet. Jenny, according to her mother, varied her manipulative techniques to fit the situation. When she wanted candy from Grandma, she asked in a "polite voice," "please Baba candy." When she wanted her Daddy to read to her, she cuddled up on his lap and gave him a hug.

Because two year olds are able to recognize and respond to the special characteristics of each parent, they may begin to show favoritism. Again, this social technique is partly an honest expression of emotion and partly an attempt to play one parent against the other. Brian was perfectly happy to let his mother color pictures with him or play with his Sesame Street characters, but only daddy was allowed to read books. In Janet's home daddy could change the words to a goodnight song, but mother was not allowed to alter a single refrain. Denise suggested that her mother take a walk as soon as dad arrived home.

Adapting to the two year old's new social skills within the family is quite a challenge in itself. But most parents actually increase the pressure on children to become socialized outside the family, to join the larger world of school and peer group. Parents expect two year olds to be toilet trained, to have a semblance of table manners, to say please, thank you, and I'm sorry at the right times, to be friendly to strangers, etc.

Both parents and children are focused on social development. Children are concerned primarily with asserting themselves within the family, while parents concentrate on teaching children to behave in a way that is acceptable in the larger culture. Certainly there is an overlap between the two, but the emphasis is different. As we all realize, our behavior within the family often does not parallel our behavior outside the family.

Beyond the Immediate Family

Within the family circle parents remain the most significant adults in a two year old's life, but special relationships do develop with grandparents, aunts, and uncles. Zachary, who is an unusually sensitive and gentle child, is especially fond of his grandfather who is totally blind. He climbs up on his grandfather's lap with a handful of books. "Grandpa's eyes can't see," Zachary explains, "but Grandpa tells good stories." After his grandfather returned from a stay in the hospital, Zachary brought his doctor's kit to his grandfather's house and took out the stethoscope. "I'm Dr. Holly, Grandpa is all better now."

Two year olds may establish an intimate relationship with other adults as well. Jed, who was very eager to go to school, told his mother, "I love Miss Marilyn (his teacher), she's my friend. I'm going to see Miss Marilyn today." Because the children are better able to interact with other adults, problems with babysitters usually diminish during the third year. Children may even look forward to playing with a favorite sitter.

Separation fears have not disappeared, however, even though they have lessened. As we have pointed out in earlier chapters, it is not uncommon for two year olds to show separation fears at bedtime or at nursery school, especially if the children have experienced a very close relationship with their parents. We did run across one solution to the babysitting problem that was particularly interesting. Andrea's parents found that Andrea accepted the babysitter when she was allowed to pay her. Before leaving at night they gave the money to Andrea, with instructions to pay the babysitter before going to bed. This idea is a good example of solving a problem by taking advantage of a two year old's feelings of autonomy. Instead of feeling small and left out, Andrea felt grown up and important when her parents spent an evening away from her.

In contrast to familiar adults, most two year olds have mixed feelings about strangers. When a new person comes into the house, a common reaction is to hide behind the sofa or bury themselves in a mother or daddy's lap. If the strangers ignore them completely, the chances are that shy behavior will turn into exhibitionism. During our first visit to Brian's house he hid behind his mother for the first few minutes. They he began to race around the room, scoot under the furniture, slap at toys wildly, and even throw them across the room.

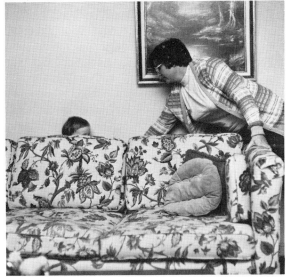

Outside of their own homes, most two year olds are friendly with strangers as long as the stranger keeps his distance. Fear of strangers who do not keep an appropriate distance, who come on too quickly, or whose appearance is different, is still very real for many two year olds. Kori dislikes any man with a moustache or a beard. Matti, who does not have a father, is frightened of a deep voice. Christopher gets hysterical when a very old neighbor comes over to visit. "Face broken," he said to his mother in an attempt to explain his fears. Once a two year old develops a fear of a particular person, it's difficult to change his mind. Often the harder the parents try to convince their child that the "frightening" person is safe, the more frightened the child becomes. Parents sometimes have a difficult time understanding the illogical fears of a two year old.

Like other people, the reaction of two year olds to new people varies with their mood and with the situation. They take an instant liking to some people and just as instantly dislike other people. They may anticipate being spoken to at the grocery store and be in a friendly mood, but be surprised and withdrawn when spoken to in the street. Despite these variations parents usually see a definite change between two and three years in the way a child interacts with other adults. The behavior of the child at the age of three differs from the the same child's behavior at two.

In general children who have just turned two are shyer, but at the same time they are more fickle in a social situation. If they are in a friendly mood, they may say "hi" to anyone. They can be enticed into performing for strangers rather easily. Three year olds, on the other hand, are more bold in their interaction, but this assertiveness may show up in a stubborn refusal to speak or a feeling of embarrassment about performing for strangers.

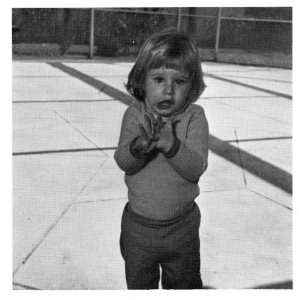

When three year olds want to interact, they are capable of initiating a conversation with strangers. Jodi, who is the youngest child in an outgoing family, had developed an elaborate greeting ritual. "Hello, how old are you? Do you have any babies at home?" Although Jodi's mother was afraid that people would consider Jodi impertinent, her greeting made perfect sense. After all most adults who attempt to start up a conversation with a young child begin with, "how old are you?" and continue with "do you have any sisters or brothers at home?"

When children first start to initiate these interactions, their plans may misfire despite good intentions. One day Erik was playing in the front yard when a couple came out of the house next door and got in their car. Erik ran over to the curb and said, "hi man, hi lady," but he got no response. As they drove away, he extended a tennis ball that was in his hand and yelled, "come back, I find a baseball."

Although two year olds are much more assertive within the family setting, they become increasingly assertive toward other adults as well. They may correct or contradict a stranger who speaks to them. When a salesman told Jason he was a smart little girl, he retorted, "I'm not a girl, I'm a boy." Later that day Jason started to whine in another store, and a salesman began to imitate him. "I don't like that noise," Jason informed the salesman in no uncertain terms.

Even when two year olds do not seem to be paying any attention to the interaction between their parents and other adults, they may be surprisingly well tuned into the social dynamics of the situation. Janice's mother told us about a visit from "Aunt Mimi." It appeared that Aunt Mimi was a stereotype spinster who made a yearly "duty" visit to every member of the family. She was basically a harmless soul but she had a habit of overstaying her welcome, and her goodbyes took as long as her visits. As Janice's mother finally bade Aunt Mimi a last goodbye, she congratulated herself silently on how patient and friendly she had been. Just at that point Janice tugged at her skirt, "Mommy, you want Aunt Mimi go home?"

Christopher embarrassed his family even more when he spoke out in front of a whole roomful of company. One of the guests started talking about a woman named Madeline. Madeline was an alcholic who lived next door, and her drinking problem was a common topic of conversation. Christopher picked up the name. "Mad-lin is a wino," he remarked in a loud voice. Christopher's mother tried to explain the remark away, but everyone knew exactly what he was saying, and where he had gotten it from. "Little pitchers have big ears," his mother reminded herself.

Although some of the time the two year old can embarrass his parents with his shyness, his assertiveness, his prejudices, or his candor, these moments of embarrassment do not occur very often. For the most part the two year old is perfectly delightful in a social situation. Erik was tossing a ball in a box when a woman came in from a neighboring apartment. "You want a turn?" Erik asked politely. The visitor flushed with surprise. "Can't I have more than one Erik, I'll never get the ball in the basket with just one turn." "No," Erik insisted, "just one turn." Then he quietly picked up the box and placed it closer to the visitor.

NEW DISCOVERIES

Space, Time and Number Two years old is a very special time in the life of children. As infants they have learned about the permanence of objects. Rattles, bottles, and people continue to exist even if they can't be seen or touched. Now at two years old children are developing another critical insight about the permanence of the world. Space and time extend beyond the boundaries of their immediate experience. There are places out there where they have never been, and things are going to happen that have not happened before.

The awareness that far away places or unknown places exist shows up in different ways. For example, Heath and Colby yelled, "Grandma's" every time they saw the Wild Kingdom on television. Grandma was not a part of the Wild Kingdom, but she did live in Omaha, and the twins knew that the program was sponsored by Mutual of Omaha. Two year olds may be curious about people who get on planes and disappear into the sky, or they may note that the sun seems to sink in to some distant hole at night.

Just as a two year old's vision of space expands, so does his sense of time. "I rode a horse last night," Melissa told us when we visited her house. "She means the merry-go-round at the carnival," her mother explained, "and it wasn't really last night, it was a couple of weeks ago."

Despite her inaccuracy Melissa had made a critical distinction. She was able to indicate that the horse ride had not been a part of the current day's events. Most two year olds anticipate the daily schedule with ease. They know when it is time to eat, time to watch T.V., time for brothers and sisters to come home, and time to go to bed. These events occur regularly every day, and together they define the notion of a day. Once this concept is in place, time can be oriented in terms of days.

Helaine especially liked to go to the bowling alley with her mother on Thursdays. The first thing she asked her mother every morning was "bowling day?" Helaine had learned to think of time in terms of days but not weeks. Since bowling occurred regularly, she hoped that each day would be the one. Michael had progressed a bit further. He had linked two days together. On Tuesday nights Michael's mother went out to a class, and on Wednesday Michael went to a play group. Instead of asking every morning about Shawn, his play group friend, Michael waited until the morning after the babysitter. He had learned that first came the babysitter and them came Shawn.

The time words that two year olds use reflect their limited conceptual framework. Melissa was not necessarily confused when she described an experience several weeks in the past as "last night." Like other two year olds, she used "last night" to refer to any past event. Lacking a system for combining days into larger units, she had no alternative. Things happened either today, a day in the past, or a day in the future, for which Melissa used "in a couple days." Some children use yesterday and tomorrow as all purpose terms. Jason had a relatively sophisticated time language in which there were separate terms for near and distant past and for near and distant future. "Last night" covered the last few nights, and "a long time ago" referred to a week or more in the past. In the same way "tomorrow" referred to the near future and "someday" to more long range prospects.

The appearance of these terms makes it possible for two year olds to talk about time. In turn parents find it much easier to talk to the children about the past and the future. However, these terms represent new concepts that are just emerging, and it is of no concern if a two year old does not use them. Even without special words for the past and the future, the child will be learning to pattern time in units larger than a day.

Ultimately the organization of space and time depends on number concepts. Space and time are quantified in phrases like "three miles away" and "ten minutes ago." Although two year olds may pick up a random phrase here and there, the application of numbers to space and time is way beyond them. However, they are beginning to be aware of number concepts in other ways.

Numbers probably are mentioned most frequently in connection with age. Children learn to hold up two fingers when asked how old they are, or perhaps three if they want to indulge in a bit of wishful thinking. But certainly it will be a long time before the children understand that they are talking about two years.

Although a child does not grasp the meaning of two years, he may understand the idea of two fingers. Fingerplays and other informal games help establish the twoness of the human body—two eyes, two ears, two hands, two feet. Pairing objects is almost an instinct with people, and two year olds are no exception. Carrying one object in the right hand and another object in the left hand is a natural way to make two. Jason surprised his parents one day by placing two hairbrushes he was carrying on the floor and announcing "two." Soon afterwards he found two shoes to carry, two toothbrushes, two trucks, etc.

Recognizing two is more of a visual accomplishment than an act of counting. Two year old children may learn to recognize other visual numbers in the same way, like five fingers on a hand or four wheels on a car. There is a mathematical regularity in any environment that can be recognized visually if encouraged by parents.

In addition to recognizing certain quantities, many two year olds begin to count. Gillian was especially attracted to the animated counting sequences on Sesame Street. The machine gun rhythm, which Gillian's parents found nerve racking, invariably caught her attention. When her father introduced the idea of counting the buttons on a new dress he was pleased to find that Gillian responded enthusiastically.

Counting seems to have gained greatly in popularity since the appearance of Sesame Street. Not only have parents become more aware of teaching children to count, but the children see a point to counting. Because of its association with the razzle dazzle on T.V., counting has become a fun social activity. Traditionally the fun of counting was emphasized by rhymes like "one, two, buckle my shoe." But Sesame Street has shown us an even more powerful technique: shout and count. There are a number of excellent books being published that are designed to introduce counting to young children.

This early counting tends to be rote; that is, it is a language exercise in which children merely repeat number words in the proper sequence. Rote counting is not necessarily accurate. A child may skip some objects while counting others more than once. Even the rote sequence may be confused. Jason started with five instead of one. Gillian always left out seven.

With enough practice and assistance two year old children can learn to count accurately. We watched Donald's mother help Donald touch each picture in a counting book as they counted out loud together. Beverly's mother had taught her to pick up each object and move it when counting, so that no object would be missed or double counted.

Gradually the children learn to count rationally. They understand the idea that each object should be counted only once and they are able to count a variety of objects in different arrangements. The transition from rote to rational counting is not an instantaneous process. The two coexist, with rational counting being used when a small quantity is involved and rote counting taking over when quantity gets too large. Barbara, for example, had learned to count the four people in her family and she could count four objects in other situations too. But when she tried to count the presents under the Christmas tree, her deliberate counting style disappeared. She touched the packages and cheerfully recited various number sequences, as if playing a private counting game.

The range of a two year old's counting skills is not very important. The difference between being able to count to three versus ten is not going to matter in the years ahead. The significance of this new concept is that children are becoming aware of quantity. They are beginning to realize that there is a systematic way to count things, whether they come in a big bunch, a small bunch, or one at a time.

New Ideas About Life

New concepts of space, time, and number help two year olds make the world more predictable and permanent. They provide a better framework for making new discoveries of all kinds. Two year old children explore a great variety of new ideas, and each child's focus of interest is different. However, one common link between these interests is the idea of life.

Two year olds are beginning to appreciate the special qualities of living things, and they see a world full of life. Natural phenomena that move dramatically may seem alive, things like the waves of the ocean, the clouds in the sky, a campfire at night. In all their forms water, wind, and fire suggest the spontaneity of life. Man made objects that move dramatically, trucks, buses and other machines, may seem to be alive. Their liveliness is enhanced by the impressive noises that enimate from them. Above all, two year olds are attracted to animals as another

form of life: attracted, and yet apprehensive too, for animals are both exciting and frightening.

The animals two year olds know best are family pets. A family pet is accepted as a member of the family, and two year olds develop a special relationship with this "brother" or "sister". For one thing the pet has the least privileges in the family. All sorts of restrictions are placed on its behavior, and the two year old is the first one to enforce these special rules. "Mittens, you bad boy", scolded Jodi, "You get off the table." Chris took even greater delight when "Pooh" jumped on a visitor's lap. "Dad," he reported excitedly, "Pooh is bugging our company."

Without question the two year old's style is to boss or control the family pet. The primary means of controlling a pet is to handle it—to pet and poke it, to hug and kiss it, to carry it around. Yet behind this bossiness is a desire to make friends, to form a personal relationship with the pet. Laura insisted on taking her dog into the bathroom with her. Jason cried when the cat would not sit next to him and watch television.

Because young children try so hard to make friends with family pets, parents often find themselves explaining the need to be gentle. Being too rough with a pet may hurt it. On the other hand the animal may hurt the child by biting or scratching. This is not an easy lesson to learn. It takes time to learn the proper way to handle a cat or a dog. However, many two year olds do learn to treat pets with greater gentleness.

Two year olds also are interested in extending their animal friendships. Birds are one of the most common animals in any environment, and it is not unusual for a two year old to chase a duck or a pigeon. Although the child enjoys the chase, the real object is to catch, or at least touch, the bird and make friends. Erik could not understand why the ducks at the park always ran away from him. The idea that they were afraid of him came as a new insight. However, the ducks would eat the bread he threw to them. Feeding an animal is another way to make contact, and children's petting zoos are ideal for this purpose.

Although two year olds enjoy touching, and feeding a variety of animals, there still is a strong element of fear. Kori, who was familiar with the family dog, was reluctant to pet her cousin Jennifer's cat. "Why don't you help Jennifer pet Isaac?" Jennifer's mother suggested to Kori. "I really don't think I should," Kori rationalized, "I have a cold."

One way to relate to animals without taking a chance is through an imaginative experience. Even two year olds who have little opportunity to meet real animals, or who are afraid of real animals, enjoy listening to an animal story. Usually these animals are personified. They talk, wear clothes, and eat human food. "Do lions really like carrot stew?", Andy asked his mother after reading a typical animal story.

Animal stories do not teach children much about animals, but they do speak to one of our deepest feelings—the desire to communicate with other animals. Two year olds talk to animals as if they will be understood, and we like to do the same. Sooner or later, however, we find ourselves telling the children that the animals cannot understand us because they do not talk. We should not reject the possibility too quickly though, for communciating with animals is such a persistent fantasy that someday people may learn how to make it come true. Someday everybody may be able to talk to the birds like St. Francis.

The lack of language is the most striking difference between animals and people, but some two year olds may notice other ones. Kori told her mother, "Kim (a dog) has no hands." For several months Kori pursued the subject as she tried to figure out whether dogs, dolls, T.V. characters and animals in her books had hands.

"Peter and Cottontail have hands cause they folding up the hankerchief."

"Grover can't open the door, cause he don't have any hands."

It seems to us that parents play an essential role in helping two year olds relate to animals. Without guidance and assistance children may become excessively fearful of animals, overly abusive, or both. Although two year olds are only beginning to appreciate the variety of animal life around them, it is an appropriate time for parents to encourage a respect for life.

Of all the families in our study Benjie and Jamie's parents expressed this feeling most clearly. During our visit Benjie found a bug outside and smashed it with a loud cry. His mother reminded him that he was not supposed to kill a bug until after he asked his parents if it was a good bug or a bad bug. Spiders were "good bugs". Recently Jamie had found several dead spiders in the house and commented, "Daddy's spiders are dead." Jamie knew that his father encouraged spiders to live in the house. On another occasion the boys had collected some snails in a can. Their father noticed one of the snails crawling out of the can and said to the boys, "Look, the snail is trying to go home." He persuaded Benjie and Jamie to put the can on the porch so all the snails could go home, and by the next morning they were gone.

Just as two year olds are beginning to recognize a wider range of life, they also are becoming more aware of the life process itself. They are most aware that animals, including people, move and eat. In addition they sometimes are exposed to the idea that life is a process of renewal, of birth and death. Questions about birth and death are inspired by direct experience. Jodi, for example, was very curious about the new baby born in her family, and was verbal enough to put her puzzlement into words: "Mommy, did I drink from your nipples when I was a baby? What did I do when I was inside you?"

Questions about death are less common because families try to shield children from this fact of life. When a death does occur in the immediate family, however, some two year olds pursue the subject. After the death of his grandmother, Jed asked over and over again when they were going to get grandma back. His mother explained the best she could but the questions still continued. Finally, she gave him a picture of his grandmother to keep by his bed, and he seemed to be satisfied. Daren found his own method of coming to terms with a grandparent's death. He had asked no questions during the funeral, and his family took it for granted that he really wasn't aware of what was going on. Then his mother noticed him drawing intently on a small slate. "I making grandpa" he said to himself as he made some circular squiggles. After several minutes, he picked up the chalk eraser, rubbed the slate vigorously, and continued with his monologue, "where Grandpa go?" "Grandpa all gone."

Summary As two year olds gain new insights into themselves and other people, and as they experience the whole range of human emotions, they are forming a sense of themselves as individual people. They are also developing a set of expectations about the world and the people in it. The way children conceive themselves to be and the expectations they hold will shape their future as much as any other factor. Expecting joy they will find it, expecting beauty they will recognize it, and expecting love they will experience it.

The two year old's new awareness of time and space adds a certain intensity to daily life. On the one hand the children are threatened by dangers that may lurk out there in unknown places, and they worry about things that might happen. On the other hand they are gaining a new sense of power and control. Knowing the difference between things that have happened and things that will happen enables them to use past experiences to make judgments about the future. A trip to the shoe store isn't scary any more because last time they got a balloon. Good experiences provide happy memories and joyful expectations.

Because the child from two to three years old is learning so many new things, as we parents are faced with an awesome responsibility and a magnificent opportunity. We can help our children feel confident about themselves and their ability to cope with new situations. We can help our children discover a wider world by providing a secure home base. Perhaps most important of all, we as parents can provide our children with a reservoir of happy memories. Sometimes the very best thing to do is turn our back on the future and focus on the here and now. For with every moment of joy and with every exposure to beauty, we are building memories for our children.